Mentoring and Coaching in Education

ALSO AVAILABLE FROM BLOOMSBURY

Mentoring and Coaching in Early Childhood Education,
edited by Michael Gasper and Rosie Walker

Effective Teacher Development, Bob Burstow

Managing Staff for Improved Performance, David Middlewood and Ian Abbott

Reflective Teaching in Primary Schools, Andrew Pollard and Dominic Wyse with Ayshea Craig, Caroline Daly, Sarah Seleznyov, Sinead Harmey, Louise Hayward, Steve Higgins and Amanda McCrory

Reflective Teaching in Secondary Schools, Andrew Pollard and Caroline Daly with Katharine Burn, Steve Higgins, Aileen Kennedy, Margaret Mulholland, Jo Fraser-Pearce, Mary Richardson, Dominic Wyse and John Yandell

Sustainable School Leadership, Mike Bottery, Wong Ping-Man and George Ngai

Learning to Lead for Transformation, Emmanuel Ngara

Understanding Educational Leadership, edited by Steven J. Courtney, Helen M. Gunter, Richard Niesche and Tina Trujillo

Developing the Expertise of Primary and Elementary Classroom Teachers, Tony Eaude

Mentoring and Coaching in Education

A Guide to Coaching and Mentoring Teachers at Every Stage of Their Careers

Lizana Oberholzer and Derek Boyle

BLOOMSBURY ACADEMIC
LONDON • NEW YORK • OXFORD • NEW DELHI • SYDNEY

BLOOMSBURY ACADEMIC
Bloomsbury Publishing Plc
50 Bedford Square, London, WC1B 3DP, UK
1385 Broadway, New York, NY 10018, USA
29 Earlsfort Terrace, Dublin 2, Ireland

BLOOMSBURY, BLOOMSBURY ACADEMIC and the Diana logo are
trademarks of Bloomsbury Publishing Plc

First published in Great Britain 2024

Copyright © Lizana Oberholzer and Derek Boyle, 2024

Lizana Oberholzer and Derek Boyle have asserted their right under the Copyright, Designs and Patents Act, 1988, to be identified as Author of this work.

For legal purposes the Acknowledgements on p. xv constitute
an extension of this copyright page.

Cover design: Grace Ridge
Cover image © PM Images / Getty Images

All rights reserved. No part of this publication may be reproduced or transmitted in any form or by any means, electronic or mechanical, including photocopying, recording, or any information storage or retrieval system, without prior permission in writing from the publishers.

Bloomsbury Publishing Plc does not have any control over, or responsibility for, any third-party websites referred to or in this book. All internet addresses given in this book were correct at the time of going to press. The author and publisher regret any inconvenience caused if addresses have changed or sites have ceased to exist, but can accept no responsibility for any such changes.

A catalogue record for this book is available from the British Library.

A catalog record for this book is available from the Library of Congress.

ISBN: HB: 978-1-3502-6423-6
PB: 978-1-3502-6422-9
ePDF: 978-1-3502-6424-3
eBook: 978-1-3502-6425-0

Typeset by Integra Software Services Pvt. Ltd.
Printed and bound in Great Britain

To find out more about our authors and books visit www.bloomsbury.com
and sign up for our newsletters.

Contents

List of Figures vii
List of Tables viii
About the Authors ix
Foreword x
How to Use This Book xii
Acknowledgements xv

Introduction 1

1 **What Is Mentoring and What Is Coaching and Why?** 5

2 **Mentoring and Coaching Initial Teacher Trainees** 23

3 **Mentoring and Coaching Newly Qualified Teachers and Early Careers Teachers** 43

4 **Mentoring and Coaching Recently Qualified Teachers/Early Careers Teachers** 61

5 **Mentoring and Coaching Middle Leaders** 79

6 **Mentoring and Coaching Senior Leaders** 101

7 **Mentoring and Coaching Headteachers** 121

8 **Mentoring and Coaching Women in Leadership** 137

9   **Mentoring and Coaching BAME Colleagues in Education and into Leadership**   155

Conclusion   169

Index   171

Figures

1.1 Phases in the mentee and mentor relationship: An adaptation of Clutterbuck and Lane's Model (2005)   10

1.2 The Dreyfus model: An adaptation of the Dreyfus model (2004)   11

1.3 Directive and non-directive behaviours: An Adaptation of Thomson (2013) and Downey's (2014) models   18

2.1 A model that could be used to develop critically reflective practice: An adaption of the spiral of enquiry model proposed by Bruner (1965) and the GROW model proposed by Whitmore (2017)   37

2.2 Encouraging your trainee to engage with self-initiated enquiry by Bruner (1965)   38

3.1 Maynard and Furlong's (1995) model of professional growth and development phases of teacher trainees   52

4.1 Buck (2020) and Thompson's (2013) mentoring continuum   64

4.2 An adaptation of the action learning set reflection tool by Brockban and Mcgill (2003)   66

5.1 An adaptation of Blanchard et al.'s (2018) situational leadership model   81

5.2 A model utilising the idea of mentoring and coaching behaviours being on continuum (Blanchard et al., 2018)   82

5.3 Four types of middle leaders   83

8.1 Drake's (2017) narrative coaching model   142

Tables

3.1　Levels of mentoring an adaptation from Bleach (2016)　　51

3.2　Levels of mentoring including opportunities for reflection an adaptation from Bleach (2016)　　52

5.1　Six elements of psychological well-being (Westerhof and Keyes 2009)　　97

5.2　Mentors and coaches' responses to elements of social well-being　　98

9.1　A tool to help colleagues identify strengths and areas for improvement　　164

About the Authors

Dr. Lizana Oberholzer

Lizana is a senior lecturer in teacher education at the University of Wolverhampton, UK. She is the programme Lead for the International MA in Education, as well as the National Professional Qualifications in School Leadership at the University of Wolverhampton. She is passionate about teacher development and is the BERA special interest group convenor for Teacher Education in England, APPG SIG convenor for Teacher Development and CPD, BELMAS research interest group convenor for governing and governance, BAMEed trustee, CMI Fellow, Chartered College of Teaching Founding Fellow, Principal Fellow of the Higher Education Academy, CollectiveEd Fellow, Chair of the UCET CPD Forum, and MAT director. Lizana is the Vice Chair of the IPDA Internatioanl Committee, as well as the Chair of the IPDA England Committee.
@LO_EduforAll

Derek Boyle

Derek has been the SCITT director at Bromley Schools' Collegiate, UK, since September 2013, but prior to this, he worked in a variety of teaching roles across a number of different schools in Kent. Originally qualifying as a physics teacher, he has also worked as an advanced skills teacher in Medway and as an assistant head teacher in Tonbridge, with pastoral, vocational and careers guidance areas of responsibility. During his time as an assistant head teacher, he had the privilege to work with the link governors from the school and play a significant role in peer mentoring.
@Bromley_SC

Foreword

The central tenet of this book is about the benefit of creating supportive, enabling relationships between professional colleagues. Whether we are considering the needs of a teacher newly arrived in the profession or a colleague recently promoted to a leadership role, the idea of establishing a formal space and time for trusted reflection and conversation is one of empowering the flourishing of others.

Throughout my career I have been fortunate enough to benefit from working alongside some amazing colleagues who have generously acted as mentor, coach or a combination of both. These were colleagues who helped me with practical tasks such as providing me with a model school improvement plan, and also who willingly gave up their time to actively listen whilst I talked myself through key decisions.

When I was preparing for headship, I was told that leadership would be a lonely business. This gave me pause – did I really want to take on a role where I would be isolated, left alone to suffer the consequences of decisions taken? I knew that I would always lead best when I could do this through collaboration. For this reason, seeking out mentoring and coaching partnerships has always been part of my leadership. As a headteacher, I was extremely fortunate to work with a professional coaching colleague who was a member of our governing body. My sessions with Barry usually took place offsite and were always exhausting but deeply rewarding. Barry's skill was to model active listening, to occasionally check for understanding, to reflect back to me insights that I revealed during our session. I met with him every half term and I can honestly say that he skilfully helped me to articulate my next leadership steps. He really made me feel that my ideas were important and always helped me to align these with my core values. I attribute much of my success as a school leader to the contribution that my coach made.

Moving to the Chartered College of Teaching as a chief executive was a big step. Again, I have been so fortunate to benefit from colleagues who were willing to advise, willing to listen and ready to help. It was through the wisdom of others, both advising and listening, that I have been able to navigate a path through our complex education system to build firm foundations for our professional body.

During research for 'Creating Learning without Limits' (2012), I met regularly with a group of academics, one of whom became my mentor. I sought to test out my thinking with her, to share stories from school that I thought would gain her approval, to constantly strive to gain her praise. This was a very different role from that of my coach. My mentor perpetually challenged my thinking, forced me to answer difficult questions and helped push forward my understanding of pedagogy and assessment practice. Within these pages we see the benefits of both mentoring and coaching from the perspective of the mentee and from the mentor. As my career has moved forward, I have seen how important it is to provide support for others as well as being ready to ask for help and to receive advice.

Teaching is a hugely demanding role. This book offers us the opportunity to consider how best we can support one another. Collegiality should always be at the heart of our profession, and the skills of coaching and mentoring absolutely embody this.

Dame Alison Peacock
Chief Executive Chartered College of Teaching, UK

How to Use This Book

The book sets out to provide mentors and coaches in school contexts with guidance and advice on how to best support professional learners in their care. It explores key literature and reflects on how the various theories and research need to be considered in the light of the professional learner's learning journey from the initial teacher training phase and early careers teacher phase all the way to leadership roles.

This book aims to provide insights on how to consider the learning journey of professional learners, in regard to their professional journey. Each chapter provides an outline of the stage the professional learner would be at and what considerations, in the light of the research and theory, need to be made to support the professional learner well. The authors argue that in this text, it is imperative to note that there is no one-size-fits-all approach and that it is the mentor, coach or teacher educator's role to evaluate and fully understand the needs of the professional learner, and to draw on the appropriate mentoring or coaching techniques and strategies based on the support of the research and theory provided. Although the book is centred in the English context, the principles and recommended practices outlined in this book can be applied within a wide range of educational contexts. However, in many cases, this book aligns with the most recent frameworks and policy changes within England and covers how mentoring and coaching need to be positioned to respond to these changes in line with the support required for the professional learner.

Each chapter sets out to provide a detailed outline of what considerations mentors and coaches need to make to enable them to support professional learners in each of the potential phases of their learning journey. The authors acknowledge that this is not an exhaustive outline of potential roles within school contexts, but the book aims to provide an outline of the key potential phases of the teacher's journey and how these can be supported. The reformed National Professional Qualifications (NPQs) (DfE, 2021) provide new development opportunities for roles such as behaviour and culture, leading teacher development and leading teaching. These roles will be explored in some of the chapters focusing on middle leadership and senior leadership, for example.

Chapter 1 outlines what mentoring and coaching are and how mentoring and coaching needs to be considered in the light of the needs of the coachee. The chapter provides an outline of key definitions, and it discusses current thinking on how mentors and coaches need to move on the continuum of coaching and mentoring to support professional learners.

Chapter 2 discusses how mentors and coaches need to reflect on the initial learning journey of a professional learner, and how the learning curriculum and the needs of the learner need to be explored.

Chapter 3 explores how the learning journeys of newly qualified teachers' (NQTs)/ Early Careers Teachers (ECTs) need to continue post their initial learning in their Initial Teacher Education year. For the purpose of the book, Initial Teacher Education will be referred to as Initial Teacher Training (ITT) as most of the key policies and texts refer to ITT. However, the authors acknowledge that, as stated by Lofthouse (2018, p. 4), using initial teacher training as a term can be 'reductive', as the term does not acknowledge the intricacies and nuances as well as the complexities of the professional learner's learning journey within the education landscape. The learning journey of the newly qualified teacher needs to be considered within the context and framework of the Early Careers Framework (DfE, 2019) as part of the DfE's teacher retention strategy.

Chapter 4 continues to explore the learning journey of the early careers teacher (ECT) as a recently qualified teacher (RQT), beyond the NQT year, and it outlines the key considerations mentors and coaches need to make to support professional learners, to continue to deepen their learning, and start preparing for next steps in relation to their career. Many NQTs tend to progress into leadership roles shortly after their NQT year, or shortly after their RQT year, and their support needs to be aligned to their specific needs and career choices within the Early Careers Framework (ECF).

Chapter 5 explores how ECT and others can start to progress on the leadership ladder and how mentoring and coaching needs to be embedded into their practice on their new journey too. Often at this stage, support is not fully in place, and the authors argue that mentoring and coaching need to be part of the professional learning journey toolkit for all teachers throughout their career, not just when they are struggling or finding the journey more challenging.

Chapter 6 reflects on how mentoring and coaching can be utilized to first support new senior leaders, and how coaching in particular can be drawn upon to help senior leaders to unlock their potential.

Chapter 7 continues to explore how future headteachers need to be supported at the novice stage of this role and, as they become more proficient, how a coaching approach can enable them to flourish and grow.

Chapter 8 explores the role mentoring and coaching play in supporting women into leadership roles in education. This chapter sets out to address core issues in relation to the representation of women in senior leadership roles in education, the challenges they face and how mentoring and coaching can provide ways forward.

Chapter 9 outlines the role mentoring and coaching plays in supporting educators from Black, Asian and Minority Ethnic (BAME) Groups into leadership roles in education. The chapter aims to address core issues in relation to the representation of BAME Groups in senior leadership roles in education, the challenges they face and how mentoring and coaching can provide ways forward.

Conclusion: In the conclusion, the authors outline how mentoring and coaching can be drawn on across the education landscape to shape strong learning conversations and to continue to grow and develop effective communities and learning, where collaborative professionalism is strengthened to ensure that teachers and future leaders can flourish and grow and positively impact the communities they serve.

References

DfE (2021), *National Professional Qualification (NPQ) Framework*. UK: DfE. Available at: National professional qualifications frameworks: from autumn 2021 – GOV.UK (www.gov.uk) (Accessed: 03. 08.2021).

Lofthouse, R. M. (2018), 'Re-imagining mentoring as a dynamic hub in the transformation of initial teacher education: The role of mentors and teacher educators'. *International Journal of Mentoring and Coaching in Education*, 7(3), pp. 248–60. doi: 10.1108/IJMCE-04-20170033.

Acknowledgements

The authors would like to thank all their family members who contributed to their learning and all their colleagues over the years who acted as mentors for them, allowing them to unlock their potential and enabling them to share their knowledge, expertise and experiences in this book. Special thanks to those who also contributed case studies to the book as well as their guidance and support. A special thanks to the editorial team for their kind support and guidance throughout the journey.

Lizana Oberholzer would like to particularly thank Harry Dodds in his capacity as a mentor, coach, supervisor, tutor, friend and colleague and for his guidance throughout her learning journey. Harry was an inspiration to all, and he will be dearly missed by many. Harry was a gentle giant and a true gentleman who lived the values of being a mentor and coach on a daily basis to help enable others. His contributions to the development of others had a profound impact on the profession and all those who were privileged to work with him.

Derek Boyle would like to thank his father, Alexander Joseph Boyle, for being a mentor and an inspiration throughout his time with us, and to Stephen Bovey, who had the faith and trust in him to appoint him to his first senior leadership position. Stephen's gentle but firm leadership style still inspires him today. Both of these wonderful mentors are missed by everyone who knew them.

Introduction

At the time of writing this book, Initial Teacher Training (ITT), Early Careers Teachers and School Educational Leadership development saw a wide range of new frameworks being implemented to help support the development of new teachers, as well as offer support for teachers continuing to develop on their journeys, as Early Career Teachers and beyond. In England the Department for Education (DfE) recognized the important role mentoring can play in supporting future teachers during their Initial Teacher Training year, early career development stages and beyond in the department's ITT Core Content Framework (DfE, 2019) and the Early Careers Framework (DfE, 2019), which outlines the DfE's road map to strategically address teacher retention.

This book aims to outline how mentoring and coaching, with the above new initiatives and frameworks in mind, can be used to support teachers from their initial training and throughout their future career development to allow them to grow and flourish as teachers, fellow mentors and school leaders. The authors argue that mentoring and coaching need to be considered a key part of the teacher and school leader's continuous professional development and learning toolkit and that, as professional learners, mentoring and coaching need to become part of the development package for teachers and leaders at all levels. Mentoring and coaching should not just be drawn on when teachers are training or are perceived to be 'struggling' (Culshaw, 2019). Lofthouse et al. (2010, p. 7) state that

> *coaching in schools takes various forms but is commonly conceived as a means of providing personalised professional support to teachers through discussion about their practice.*

Mentoring and coaching need to be welcomed in education, as it is in industry, as a part of every teacher and leader's learning portfolio that enables them to continue to reflect and deepen their own learning throughout their career alongside the support of a mentor or an experienced coach, who can help frame learning conversations and reflections in a safe space. Kline (2010) highlights the importance of having think partners that can enable others to grow, and Knight (2016) outlines the importance of teachers and educators engaging in better learning conversations in school contexts.

This book aims to outline how these conversations can be utilize to help make the most of every teacher or leader's talents (Whitmore, 2017).

According to Ofsted (2020), 'Effective mentoring and a well-paced curriculum are key to high quality initial teacher education', and the authors argue that the same is true of developing teachers throughout their careers. The Carter Review (2015) points out mentoring practices need to be more consistent, and as a result, the mentor standards were published (DfE, 2016) to provide mentors with a means to self-evaluate their practice and to strengthen their practices more. However, the Carter Review, like Lofthouse et al. (2010), also acknowledges that more time is needed for mentors and coaches to ensure that they are able to support others well through effective and supportive learning conversations. This book explores how these conversations can be shaped and aims to support mentors in the important work that they set out to do with colleagues and peers to continue to build a strong learning community. The book does not endeavour to advocate a particular style or approach of mentoring or coaching; it also does not draw on the frameworks for ITT and ECF, which advocates that mentoring and coaching need to work through the teacher standards as mapped out in these frameworks. Instead, the book advocates, that mentors and coaches need to fully understand the needs of their mentees and coachees, to enable them to draw on their mentoring and coaching toolkit, to utilize the most appropriate strategies and approaches to meet the professional learners' needs.

Although the book is mainly centred in the English context, the principles and concepts explored within the book can be used across practices and contexts, and the authors show that these provide mentors and coaches with a strong foundation to support others on their learning journey.

References

Culshaw, S. Y. (2019), *An Exploration of What It Means to Be Struggling as a Secondary Teacher in England*. UK: University of Hertfordshire. Available: 15030978 CULSHAW Suzanne Final Version of PhD Submission.pdf (herts.ac.uk) (Accessed: 01.06.2021).

Department for Education (2015), 'Carter review of initial teacher training'. Available: https://www.gov.uk/government/publications/carter-review-of-initial-teacher-training (Accessed: 01.06.2021).

Department for Education (2016), 'National Standards for School-Based Initial Teacher Training (ITT) Mentors'. Available at: https://assets.publishing.service.gov.uk/government/uploads/system/uploads/attachment_data/file/536891/Mentor_standards_report_Final.pdf (Accessed: 01.06.2021).

Department for Education (2019), 'Early Career Framework: A Framework of Standards to Help Early Career Teachers Succeed at the Start of Their Careers'. Available at: Early career framework – GOV.UK (www.gov.uk) (Accessed: 01.06.2021).

Department for Education (2021), 'National professional qualifications (NPQs) reforms'. Available at: https://www.gov.uk/government/publications/national-professional-qualifications-npqs-reforms/national-professional-qualifications-npqs-reforms (Accessed: 01.06.2021).

Kline, N. (2010), *Time to Think: Listening to Ignite the Human Mind*. UK: Cassell Publishing.

Knight, J. (2016), *Better Conversations: Coaching Ourselves and Each Other to Be More Credible, Caring and Connected*. London: Corwin Press.

Lofthouse, R., Leat, D. and Towler, C. (2010), *Coaching for Teaching and Learning: A Practical Guide for Schools*. UK: National College for School Leadership.

Ofsted (2020), *Effective Mentoring and a Well-Paced Curriculum Are Key to High Quality Initial Teacher Education*. UK: Ofsted. Available at: https://www.gov.uk/government/news/effective-mentoring-and-a-well-paced-curriculum-are-key-to-high-quality-initial-teacher-education (Accessed: 01.06.2021).

Whitmore, J. (2017), *Coaching for Performance*. London: Brealey.

1

What Is Mentoring and What Is Coaching and Why?

Lizana Oberholzer and Rachel Lofthouse

In some educational contexts mentoring and coaching are used interchangeably, and it is therefore important to ensure that there is a clear understanding of what is meant by coaching and mentoring throughout the book, and how mentoring and coaching can be utilized to support others. For each chapter we shall aim to set out specific aims and objectives, and the key areas of focus for this chapter are outlined below.

This chapter sets out to:

- Provide clear definitions for coaching and mentoring,
- Explore how coaching and mentoring can be used in schools to develop staff,
- What to consider when coaching or mentoring,
- What skills to develop when coaching or mentoring,
- Explore the evolution of the mentoring relationship,
- Show how to draw on the continuum of mentoring and coaching.

What Are Coaching and Mentoring?

The European Mentoring and Coaching Council (EMCC, 2016) points out that when contracting with a mentee or coachee, it is imperative to be clear on what the differences are between mentoring and coaching. The guidance states that a mentor or coach needs to 'explain and strive to ensure that the client and sponsor know and fully understand the nature, terms, and conditions of the coaching, and mentoring'. 'Client' refers to the mentee or coachee who will engage with the support, and 'sponsor' within this context will refer to the school or education context supporting the coaching and mentoring being put in place. Understanding the 'nature' of mentoring and coaching refers to (a) the differences between coaching and mentoring in relation to their functions and disciplines, and (b) how it will facilitate learning conversations and thinking.

With this in mind, this section of the book aims to unpack the differences between mentoring and coaching to ensure that when the authors refer to mentoring and coaching there is clarity on (a) what it is, (b) its purpose and (c) how it aims to facilitate learning conversations.

What Is Mentoring?

Hughes (2003) points out that mentoring is about 'telling', providing others with guidance and advice. Connor and Pokora (2016) highlight that mentoring and coaching are both learning relationships. Starr (2013) states that the mentor's role is to provide guidance and advice and that the role is often anchored in the mentor's expertise. Roberts (2010, p. 162) reflects that mentoring is a 'formalised process whereby a more knowledgeable and experienced person actuates a supportive role of overseeing and encouraging reflection and learning with a less experienced and knowledgeable person, so as to facilitate that person's career and personal development'. 'Actuate' is an interesting word choice, as it suggests to 'act' in a certain way, and the reference to 'experience' and being 'knowledgeable' suggests that there are certain expectations of mentors in how they need to engage with mentees and that there is a certain amount of 'telling' as authors such as Hughes (2003) and Thomson (2013) describe mentoring. In addition, mentors need to have the necessary skills and knowledge to support the mentee on their learning journey.

We often see examples of advice and guidance given when mentors in Initial Teacher Training (ITT), or in any other mentoring relationship, especially when the mentee is a novice (Dreyfus and Dreyfus, 2004; Enser and Enser, 2021), have to take the mentee by the hand in a more directive way. They need to do more 'telling' and giving advice through a directive learning dialogue, until the mentee progresses from the initial stages of the mentoring relationship, where rapport is built and initial direction is given, as suggested by Clutterbuck and Lane (2005) when the authors outline the phases of the mentor relationship. However, as the relationship progresses and the mentee becomes more confident, competent and proficient in their skills acquisition, the mentor relationship evolves from dependence to independence, where the mentee requires different support from those around them, and their thinking needs to be facilitated more through the use of questioning. This is when the mentor needs to recontract and negotiate the mentoring relationship to progress into a more non-directive coaching approach. We intend to explore this aspect of the mentoring relationship, and the evolution of the relationship, in more detail later in the chapter.

However, to ensure that the definitions are clear, the authors aim to frame the definitions within the context of the relationship development of the mentor and the mentee. As the relationship evolves, different approaches and practices are drawn on to stretch and challenge the mentee on their journey, and it is therefore important to acknowledge, as outlined in Curee's National Framework for Mentoring and Coaching (2003), that at times some of the key skills of mentoring and coaching do overlap. However, the authors want to stress very strongly that within the text, coaching and mentoring are defined separately and not used interchangeably.

The authors argue that mentors and coaches need to have a clear understanding of what mentoring is and what coaching is, as well as when to coach and when to mentor, to ensure that these approaches are utilized effectively to support colleagues in the most appropriate way to meet the needs of those they are supporting. When the needs of the mentee evolve to the point where coaching needs to be considered as a more appropriate approach, mentors need to feel confident to offer alternative support and approaches to continue to support the mentee well. It is important that mentors discuss this next step with the coachee and gain the appropriate consent to ensure that the relationship can progress. Coaching should never become a 'done to' process, as coachees need to drive their own learning journeys. By revisiting and agreeing the next steps in the mentoring or coaching relationship, the mentor recontracts with the mentee that they will move forward to engage in a coaching relationship.

Unfortunately, in so many contexts, coaching and mentoring are becoming aligned with performance management practices, appraisals and capability, which impact on how these supportive approaches are perceived in education contexts. Often the view is that when you are assigned a coach or mentor, you are on a 'support' plan, and coaching and mentoring practices are often viewed with suspicion and in a negative light. Alternatively, mentoring is often aligned with teacher training, but in other professions, having a sponsor as a mentor is common place to help you to progress on your learning journey and in your career (Lancer et al., 2016).

What Is Coaching?

Coaching can be defined as facilitating thinking (Van Nieuwerburgh, 2017), where the coach facilitates the learning conversation through the use of coaching models, which help frame the reflective conversation and help the coachee to unpack his or her key ideas with the aim to find possible solutions and to unlock his or her potential (Whitmore, 2017).

Thomson (2013) states that mentoring is more directive, whereas coaching is non-directive and that the coachee drives the coaching journey. The coach does not need to be an expert in the field. For the purpose of this book, mentoring will be referred to as a more directive approach where guidance and support are often anchored in the experience and subject knowledge of the mentor, whereas coaching is considered non-directive: a learning conversation which is framed through the use of coaching models to help facilitate the thinking of the coachee.

How Are Coaching and Mentoring Used in Schools to Develop Staff Currently, and How Can Coaching and Mentoring Be Reimagined in the Future?

The authors touch on the notion that mentoring and coaching are often used in schools, and other education contexts, to either train new teachers or support teachers who might be struggling. In some cases, some schools and local authorities (LAs) still provide coaching opportunities for school leaders and headteachers; however, this is not a consistent approach, and it is therefore important to discuss how we need to re-image coaching and mentoring as part of the support for a teacher or leader's professional learning journey to help them to flourish as opposed to the, at times, negative connotations associated with mentoring and coaching. In the most recent National Professional Qualifications for School Leaders, learners were required to work with a coach to help them to develop their leadership practices in schools. However, development of coaches in these roles often varies, and there is a wide range of perspectives on what this means. It is therefore more important than ever to ensure that coaches and mentors have clarity on their roles to enable them to unlock the potential in others.

Vare et al. (2021) emphasize the important role mentoring and coaching can have in professional learning development for teachers. Vare et al. (2021) point out that teachers need to engage with sustained learning opportunities that will enable them and deepen their learning, as well as give them agency. Coaching and mentoring set out to foster strong, trusting relationships and to develop strong professional learning conversations with the aim to enable others and to unlock their potential (Whitmore, 2017).

Lofthouse (2021) demonstrates through her work leading CollectiveED how, in the spirit of collaborative professionalism, coaching and mentoring can become powerful vehicles for supporting others to grow in a variety of ways (Hargreaves and O'Connor, 2018).

CollectivED, The Centre for Mentoring, Coaching and Professional Learning at Leeds Beckett University, aims to expand the available knowledge base through research on coaching and mentoring, and also to support the development of professional practices. While we acknowledge the differences between coaching and mentoring, we also recognize their shared qualities. We advocate for mentoring and coaching as collaborative conversations which create powerful professional learning and which can build the capacity of educators to create contexts that support inclusive career-long and profession-wide learning. Our research demonstrates that coaching and mentoring can increase opportunities for educational change through enhanced professional agency and well-being. Two examples illustrate these qualities: the first relates to an advanced mentoring programme of professional learning; the second comes from a research project which explored a year-long programme of headteacher coaching.

The CollectivED Advanced Mentoring programme provides a space in which mentors (from a range of contexts) form a community of practice to develop insights into mentoring, gain understanding and skills and reflect on the personal and professional attributes that mentors bring to their work. In addition to supporting Initial Teacher Education (ITE) and Early Careers Teacher (ECT) mentors, the programme also enables school leaders to develop expansive, strategic and operational thinking in relation to mentoring. Two participant primary heads of school shared their insights into mentoring in CollectivED blogposts. Both recognized that mentoring was essential in building professional capacity in school. For example, Wathen (2021) recommended that mentors ensure new teachers are inducted into their phase team to gain crucial collaborative learning experiences. She also recognized that mentoring needed to enhance new teachers' attributes and skills to enable them to find greater autonomy as they progress through their careers. Three steps to being an effective mentor are suggested by Pierce (2021): prioritising building relationships with the mentee, enabling open dialogue between the mentor and mentee and using mentoring as the basis of collaborative approaches in school.

The headteacher coaching research (Lofthouse and Whiteside, 2020; Lofthouse et al., 2021) indicated the contribution of coaching to making school leadership, and therefore the school system, more sustainable. Many of the headteachers who engaged in the research had experienced what one phrased as the 'erosion of their resilience' which had detrimental effects on their well-being and work–life balance. Headteachers said that they had feelings of extreme isolation and loneliness and experienced high levels of pressure and professional scrutiny. They felt constrained by insufficient school funds and due to workload had very little opportunity to reflect on decisions or plan ahead. This compounded the 'emotional weight' of having to provide emotional, pastoral and practical care to their school community. Coaching created a protected, sustained and supported space which gave headteachers the time to prioritize the issues that needed resolving. They felt that they had improved their ability to develop colleagues, manage difficult issues and improve working relationships as well as develop an enhanced capacity for problem-solving, strategic thinking and the need to cope with continuing demands of the job, including emergency management. They were universal in indicating that coaching had had positive impacts on their self-belief and confidence and had helped them to place a greater priority on their own physical and emotional health.

Similar Coaching and Mentoring Programmes are delivered by universities on a national level, and the University of Wolverhampton and Bromley Collegiate are examples where coaching and mentoring courses are delivered to ITE as well as school leaders. Similar to this, feedback is shared by ECT mentors and school leaders in regard to the value of coaching and mentoring support and the importance of enabling school leaders in particular to have a safe space to make sense of the challenges they face and to develop key strategies, with the aim to lead their teams with confidence.

Ofsted (2020) acknowledges the importance of effective mentoring to develop future teachers; however, the authors argue that mentoring and coaching need to be shaped to support teachers throughout their careers, as part of their development – a self-care toolkit to enable them to continue to become the teachers or leaders they need to be for their learners (Lofthouse, 2020).

What to Consider When Mentoring and Coaching

Connor and Pokora (2016) describe mentoring and coaching as learning relationships. It is important as a mentor or coach to ensure that trusting learning relationships are developed to ensure that the mentee or coachee is able to progress on their journey. Clutterbuck and Lane (2005) provide a helpful outline of how the mentor relationship's phases need to be considered:

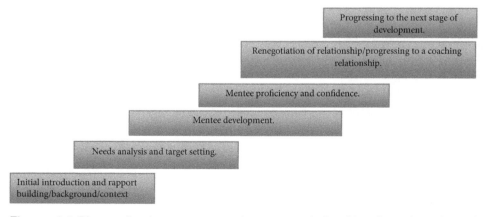

Figure 1.1 Phases in the mentee and mentor relationship: An adaptation of Clutterbuck and Lane's Model (2005).

The authors emphasize the importance of using rapport building to embed a strong trusting relationship before a more directive approach is used to guide the mentee through the learning journey (Thomson, 2013). Dreyfus (2004) outlines that when starting a new learning journey, the learner often starts as a novice and progresses to the various levels of skills acquisition as they move through the phases of their journey, as illustrated in Figure 1.2.

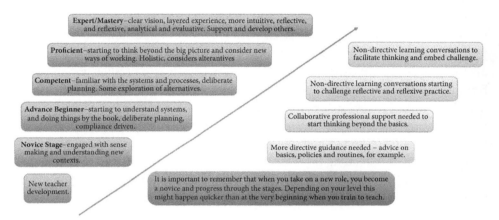

Figure 1.2 The Dreyfus model: An adaptation of the Dreyfus model (2004).

Why is it important to understand the phases of the mentor relationship and, of course, the Dreyfus Model? Mentors need to evaluate the needs of their mentees. If a mentee is at a novice stage, for example, and at the very first phases of their mentor relationship with their mentor, it is often best to first familiarize the mentee with the organisation's structures, its policies, and its rules. It is important to take the mentee through the required learning stages to get them to a point where they can confidently look up and take on more. Giving new mentees a road map, which guide them in a step-by-step way, ensures that they are nurtured and able to develop in confidence. Providing guidance, advice, resources and help at this stage will be more meaningful than to ask a range of questions, as often novices will not be aware of the answers (they simply don't know what they don't know), but they might feel that they should know what the answers are. This can impact on their confidence and, of course, also trigger a limbic response, which might result in a fight, flight or freeze reaction. Through the learning conversation, mentors need to strive for mentees to feel safe to enable them to open up to learning (Maslow, 1973). Cultivating trusting learning conversations are key (Buck, 2020; Covey, 2006).

As the mentee progresses through the journey, and work through the initial phases, they will become more competent, at which point more questions can be asked. However, the mentor still needs to maintain the balance and ensure that questions are open but explore 'what' and 'how' questions to ensure that the mentor can fully engage without triggering the mentee to become defensive in their practices (Thomson, 2013). However, as proficient or expert phases are reached, the mentor can, as suggested in the above, discuss a potential shift from a mentoring to a coaching approach with the mentee to help them to be more challenged in their practice, and 'why' questions can gradually become more common in the learning conversations. However, it is important for coaches at this stage to be mindful of how such a change to 'why' questions might impact on the coachee's confidence and ability to develop. It is a gradual progression from dependence to independence. Door (2015) points out in her work that it is also important when using a graduating approach to be mindful of the fact that the bigger picture of education, and the learning journey, is not lost and that reflections need to help the coachee explore a wide range of aspects with a wide range of theory and reading in mind. The aim is to move the learners from being reflective to reflexive, to enable them to challenge their own beliefs, which often translates into behaviours, and for these behaviours to be addressed successfully and in a sustained way. The learner needs to challenge these beliefs and refine or change them, which in turn will translate into transformative practices (Door, 2015).

What to Consider as a Mentor

Most mentors in education become involved in the mentoring process via Initial Teacher Training in England; however, some are also involved in supporting learners in schools as pastoral mentors, or school leaders. For the purpose of this book, the focus will be on teacher education, and it will therefore be appropriate to start off with exploring the mentor's role at the start of the teacher's learning journey, which is often referred to as the initial phase in England and in other contexts, as preservice teachers.

The Carter Review (DfE, 2015) outlines that mentoring needs to be more consistent. In response to this review, the National Standards for school-based initial teacher training mentors (DfE, 2016) was published. These standards provide mentors with an opportunity to work with the Initial Teacher Training providers, or their schools, to self-evaluate their needs against these standards and also to self-assess their needs and skills to strengthen their practice. One of the criticisms of the standards is that it cannot be enforced, and that mentors, and their organisations, cannot formally be held accountable for the standard of mentoring that takes place within their contexts.

Providers can of course do their own internal analysis and evaluations, but there is no formal mechanism in place to ensure that each school does it well. However, the authors see the standards as a welcome initial step to raise the importance of the mentor role and also the required quality of provision that is needed to support a mentee.

The standards outline the mentor's role as follows:

<u>Standard 1 – Personal qualities</u>

Establish trusting relationships, model high standards of practice and emphasize with the challenges a trainee faces.

<u>Standard 2 – Teaching</u>

Support trainees to develop their teaching practice in order to set high expectations and to meet the needs of all pupils.

<u>Standard 3 – Professionalism</u>

Induct the trainee into professional norms and values and help them to understand the importance of the role and the responsibilities of teachers in society.

<u>Standard 4 – Self-development and working in partnership</u>

Continue to develop their own professional knowledge, skills and understanding and invest time in developing a good working relationship within relevant ITT partnerships.

Similar to the points made above, mentors need to develop, within an initial teacher training context, trusting relationships, model practice and provide appropriate support that aims to meet the mentee's needs. They also need to help the mentee to understand how to engage with their new work environment as professionals and to understand the requirements of the role. The standards also point out that it is important for mentors to work effectively with others, to drive their own learning and to work in partnership with others.

The authors want to add that mentors need to engage with the mentor development opportunities provided for them; however, it is important to engage beyond the support provided in relation to the logistics of the mentoring role. They need to develop their own understanding of how to shape the learning journey for an adult who is placed in their care as a learner. They need to think carefully about the learning development needs of the mentee and how they can best support them.

Often when looking at national documentation, it outlines frameworks and rigorous ways of checking and managing processes. However, mentoring is more nuanced than just the checkboxes and statements outlined in the ITT Core Framework. It is a process whereby the mentor evaluates the needs of the mentee and has a real in-depth understanding of the mentee's learning needs to ensure that they are supported in the most appropriate way for them. It is often a concern that documents like the Early Careers Framework (ECF), and others, do very little to address how mentors need to understand the learning needs of the mentee and how their learning needs to be addressed. The 'Learn that …' and 'Learn how to …' statements in the ITT

Core Framework focus on what the mentee needs to learn regarding their practice, but the authors argue that there needs to be a stronger emphasis on the mentor's journey too, on how the mentee learns, to ensure that the learning they need to do can happen. The prescriptive nature of the 'Learn that …' and 'Learn how to …', and the narrow list of research, leaves little room for open learning conversations and often assumes that these are areas of focus that will be needed. However, mentee needs are often more complex than that, as they might need to develop curriculum knowledge, or want to learn more about data analysis and how it translates into planning for learner needs. It is therefore important for mentors and coaches to develop the necessary skills and toolkit to support each mentee in the best possible way.

During formal mentor training, where mentor handbooks are shared along with some of the documents and guidance, there is often a focus on the process rather than the learning. The authors argue that if there is a stronger focus on the bespoke learning needs of the mentee, and mentors/coaches are developed to keep the learning needs of their adult learner in mind, the mentee will have a stronger foundation in place. In addition to this, to ensure that appropriate learning and support are in place, the mentor needs to have a strong foundation as an expert in mentoring and a clear understanding of how adults learn, as well as a strong foundation in their own subject or phase that they work in.

Mentors need to be armed with the necessary skills and knowledge to enable them to make clear professional judgements to enable them to use their discretion to help the mentee in their care to develop. Furlong (2013) points out that the challenge for teacher education is to maintain a balance between the practical element of the teacher education curriculum and the critical elements required to help the mentor and mentee to engage deeply in their learning. Door (2015) points out that reflections require the mentee to consider a wide range of theories, reading and views and explore them critically. Mentors therefore need to be able to facilitate this thinking and critical exploration to unpack the 'why' in relation to their practice more clearly and to provide the mentee with a detailed understanding of how they need to approach their practice, what to consider and why the choices were made.

Similarly, these principles apply to mentoring new leaders into their leadership roles too. When leaders are new in their role, they too will go through a novice stage. They might be experts in their subject area but a novice in their new role. They might progress through the role to the next stages quicker, but at the start of the journey, it is key for the mentor to understand the mentee's novice status. They need to draw on their own knowledge of the learning journey to guide and support the leader well. It is therefore important to reflect on how peers or adults learn to ensure that the mentoring practice and approaches are adjusted to the needs of those being supported.

In this book, the authors do not subscribe to one mentoring or coaching model but argue instead that mentors need to develop an understanding of a wide range of frameworks, strategies and skills, similar to when they support learners in the classroom to ensure that they can draw on these to meet the needs of their mentees in an appropriate way.

It is also important as a mentor to acknowledge that your mentee develops in their own unique way and that each individual will naturally develop at their own pace. It is therefore important to have a detailed understanding of what mentoring is, how it can be used and what strategies you can draw on to support your mentee.

Once your mentoring relationship progresses to a more advanced stage, where you find that your mentee is moving towards independence and you start considering how to support them to move forward via coaching, you might want to start reflecting on how you can use coaching strategies.

What to consider as a coach

Similar to mentoring, coaching is a learning relationship (Connor and Pokora, 2017). However, the emphasis shift here is that the coachee is in control of the journey (Thomson, 2013). As outlined in the above, mentoring relationships are often complex, and in ITT, it is often also coupled with mentors having to contribute to the assessment outcomes of the mentee, and it might well be that the coaching relationship will only start after the assessment processes are finalized for the mentee. However, this is often a very useful and a natural progression into more open learning conversations, and there are a wide range of coaching models that can be drawn on to help facilitate these.

Coaching is defined as a non-directive learning conversation for the purpose of the book, and Buck's (2020, p. 20) BASIC coaching method definition develops this further as:

> ... a one-to-one conversation that focuses on the enhancement of learning through increasing self-awareness and a sense of personal responsibility, where the coach facilitates the self-directed learning of the coachee, through questioning, active listening, appropriate challenge and when needed practical guidance in a supportive and encouraging environment that leaves the coachee feeling clearer and more optimistic about the feature.

The authors feel that the reference to 'practical guidance' is important to point out, as, in a coaching context, this can only happen with the permission of the coachee, as the coachee drives the learning journey. The coach therefore needs to clarify and check with the coachee if the advice will be helpful and enable the coachee's thinking to move forward. When considering Clutterbuck and Lane's (2005) phases of the development of the mentoring relationship, the authors argue that the coaching relationship will start to develop during the winding down phrase or, when looking at the Dreyfus Model (Dreyfus, 2004), when the mentee is moving into the proficient zone of their skills development. Mentors and coaches therefore need to evaluate the needs of their mentees carefully and make professional judgements when to coach and when to mentor, opposed to a one-size-fits-all approach, where either a set mentoring model is used or, as in some cases, instructional coaching or specific coaching modes, such as the GROW (G – goal, R – reality, O – options, W – will) model, are advocated. Mentees and coachees, like the learners or teachers they support in their classrooms, have diverse needs and develop at different rates. Some mentees might have previous experience as teaching assistants or might have had different career paths as more mature learners, so might need an accelerated approach to their learning journey, whereas others might be at the very beginning and so complete novices. Similarly, leaders might have some experience from a previous career but need support on how to translate their experience into a school context, and they might therefore move quicker through the novice and advanced beginner stage, to proficiency and beyond. It is therefore important to have a range of skills and strategies to draw on to support them.

Understanding your coachee or mentee's needs

Buck (2020) and Knight (2016) stress the importance of a trusting learning relationship. Building a strong relationship with the mentee or coachee is imperative to ensure that the relationship can move forward, and it is also why it is important to have a clear sense of how professional learners learn, how they develop their skills and how the relationship between the professional learner and the mentor, and later coach, evolves. As part of that journey, it is important to reflect on the initial needs of the professional learner and to have a clear understanding of what the professional learner's starting points are.

In education, professional learners are often assigned to a mentor, and they have to work closely with this mentor during this time. At times there are relationship challenges which need to be mediated; however, these are often supported by the senior lead on staff development or, in the case of a novice teacher, by both the partnership tutor (this can be a university tutor or school-based partnership tutor) and the senior lead for staff development. There are many titles that are associated with the senior lead for staff development; in some contexts they are referred to as the Professional Tutor, Senior Mentor or ITT Coordinator. For ease, and for the purpose of the book, we shall refer to the senior lead for staff development (SLSD).

In other professions, mentors are often approached by mentees to sponsor their journey as mentioned (Lancer et al., 2016), and this is also the case with coachees. In these contexts, mentors and coaches often arrange for an initial 'chemistry' session to take place with the aim to evaluate whether both parties can collaborate and to ensure that there is an appropriate rapport in place between the professional learner and teacher educator in order to enable both parties to move forward with the learning relationship. Often in education, initial meetings do take place, but the purpose is often not to measure whether both parties can move the relationship forward; they are often taking place in the form of a brief introduction. These meetings can be utilized well when used as an opportunity to get to know the mentee better and to gain a clear understanding of their learning needs; however, often these are missed opportunities to start cementing a strong trusting relationship. Making the most of the introduction meeting is key.

A helpful tool that can be used is an initial subject audit, which the professional learner can complete prior to the meeting. The professional learner can also complete a pre-meeting questionnaire to provide the mentor with more information about themselves, their learning needs, expectations and aspirations.

For example

1. Introduce yourself to your mentor by providing a short summary of your learning journey so far (100 words).
2. Explain in 100 words why you want to become a teacher.
3. What are your personal interests?
4. What do you hope to gain from this year?
5. What do you feel are your strengths in relation to your subject knowledge?
6. What do you feel you want to continue to work on?
7. What are you hoping to gain from your mentor?
8. How do you hope to engage with your mentor?
9. What questions do you want to ask your mentor at this stage?
10. In 100 words describe the teacher you are hoping to develop into.
11. What are you looking forward to during your training year?
12. What is your favourite book?
13. What are your hobbies?
14. What else do you want to share with your mentor?

It is often also helpful to ask for a Curriculum Vitae, as it will provide a broad overview of the professional learner's experience. As a mentor or coach, it is important to look at all the necessary information prior to this initial meeting to have an informed conversation with the mentee.

The Continuum between coaching and mentoring – when to coach and when to mentor

Buck (2020) points out that it is important to know when to mentor and when to coach and that the mentor/coach needs to have a clear understanding of the needs of the professional learner. The mentor or coach needs to be able to seamlessly move on the continuum of mentoring and coaching to ensure that the mentee/coachee's needs are met in the most appropriate way to ensure that they learn best. According to Knight (2016), practices like coaching enable others to have better conversations within learning contexts. However, these conversations can only be 'better' if the mentor/coach is skilled enough to facilitate the conversation well, with a clear understanding of how to move on the continuum of mentoring and coaching to facilitate the thinking of the mentee/coachee in a safe learning space. Often slipping into the coaching mode before cementing a strong trusting relationship with the mentee can impact on trust and can move the mentee into a limbic response of fight, flight or freeze (Bentley, 2020; Buck, 2020; Covey, 2010). Developing a trusting learning relationship is key to enable the mentee/coachee to flourish from the outset (Buck, 2020).

Knowing when to push and when to pull continues to strengthen the trusting relationship and creates a safe learning space for the professional learner to enable them to progress on their learning journey. In an adaptation of Thomson (2013) and Downey (2014) outlines the directive and non-directive behaviours as follows:

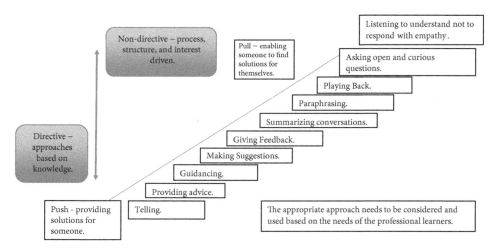

Figure 1.3 Directive and non-directive behaviours: An Adaptation of Thomson (2013) and Downey's (2014) models.

> **Reflective Task**
> - After reading this chapter, how did your new learning on the development phases of the mentoring relationship and the skills development of the professional learner you will be working with help you to understand how you need to refine your mentoring practice?
> - What changes will you make in the light of your new learning and insights?
> - How will you prepare for your first initial meeting with your mentee?
> - What will you do to create a trusting, safe learning space?

Recommended Reading

Starr, J. (2014), *The Mentoring Manual: Your Step-by-Step Guide to Being a Better Mentor*. UK: Pearson Education Limited.

Van Nieuwerburgh, C. (2012), *Coaching in Education: Getting Better Results for Students, Educators and Parents*. UK: Routledge.

Van Nieuwerburgh, C. (2017), *An Introduction to Coaching Skills: A Practical Guide*. UK: Sage.

References

Bentley, R. (2020), 'Break-through conversations', Q595. Available at: https://q595-breakthrough-conversations.com/ (Accessed: 01.09.2021).

Buck, A. (2020), *The BASIC Coaching Method: All You Need to Know to Coach with Confidence*. UK: Cadogan Press.

Clutterbuck, D. and Lane, G. (2005), *The Situational Mentor*. London: Gower.

Connor, M. and Pokora, J. (2016), *Coaching and Mentoring at Work: Developing Effective Practice*. 3rd edn. London: Open University Press.

Connor, M. and Pokora, J. (2017), *Coaching and Mentoring at Work: Developing Effective Practice*. 3rd edn. London: Open University Press.

Covey, S.M.R. (2006), *The Speed of Trust: The One Thing That Changes Everything*. UK: Simon & Schuster.

Covey, S.M.R. (2010), *The Speed of Trust: The One Thing That Changes Everything*. UK: Simon & Schuster.

Department for Education (2016), 'National Standards for School Based Initial Teacher Training Mentors, Stationery Office'. London. Available at: https://assets.publishing.service.gov.uk/government/uploads/system/uploads/attachment_data/file/536891/Mentor_standards_report_Final.pdf (Accessed: 25.09.2019).

Department for Education (2020), 'Initial teacher training (ITT): core content framework'. Available at: https://www.gov.uk/government/publications/initial-teacher-training-itt-core-content-framework (Accessed: 01.06.2021).

DfE (2015), Carter Review of Initial Teacher Training (ITT). Available: https://www.gov.uk/government/publications/carter-review-of-initial-teacher-training (Accessed: 13.10.2020).

Door, V. (2015), *Developing Creative and Critical Educational Practitioners*. UK: Critical Publishing.

Downey, M. (2014), *Effective Modern Coaching: The Principles and Art of Successful Business Coaching*. London: LID Publishing Limited.

Dreyfus, S. (2004), 'The five-stage model of adult skill acquisition'. *Bulletin of Science, Technology & Society*, 24(3) (June 2004), pp. 177–81. Available: Dreyfus-skill-level.pdf (bu.edu) (Accessed: 01.06.2021).

Durrant, J. (2020), *Teacher Agency, Professional Development and School Improvement*. Oxon: Roughtledge.

EMCC (2016), Global Code for Ethics for Coaches, Mentors, and Supervisors, EMCC. Available: Global_Code_of_Ethics_EN_v3.pdf (emccuk.org) (Accessed: 01.06.2021).

Enser, E. and Enser, M. (2021), *The CPD Curriculum: Creating Conditions for Growth*. UK: Crown House Publishing Limited.

Furlong, J. (2013), *Education – An Anatomy of the Discipline: Rescuing the University Project?* London: Routledge.

Hargreaves, A. and O'Connor, M. T (2018), *Collaborative Professionalism: When Teaching Together Means Learning for All*. UK: Corwin.

Hughes, M. (2003), *And the Main Thing Is Learning: Keeping the Focus on Learning – For Pupils and Teachers*. UK: Jigsaw Pieces.

Knight, J. (2016), *Better Conversations: Coaching Ourselves and Each Other to Be More Credible, Caring and Connected*. London: Corwin Press.

Lancer, N., Clutterbuck, D. and Megginson, D. (2016), *Techniques for Coaching and Mentoring*, 2nd edn. Oxon: Routledge.

Lofthouse, R. M. (2020), BERA Keynote: Reimagining Mentoring and Coaching Post Covid-19: Creating Professional Legacy through Mentoring – Professor Rachel Lofthouse, Delivered: 17.10.2021.

Lofthouse, R., Lofthouse, C. and Whiteside, R. (2021), 'Unlocking coaching and mentoring'. In: Hargreaves, E. and Rolls, L. (Eds.), *Unlocking Research: Reimagining Professional Development in Schools*. Routledge.

Lofthouse, R. and Whiteside, R., 2020, 'Sustaining a Vital Profession: A research report into the impact of Leadership Coaching in schools', Leeds Beckett University. Available at: https://www.leedsbeckett.ac.uk/-/media/files/schools/school-of-education/sustaining-a-vital-profession–final-report.pdf?la=en&hash=246B2F6A411111B23E9522E7220BB6BE.

Lofthouse, R. M., Rose, A. and Whiteside, R. (2022), 'Understanding coaching efficacy in education through activity systems: Privileging the nuances of provision', *International Journal of Mentoring and Coaching in Education*, Vol. 11 No. 2, pp. 153–169. ahead-of-print No. ahead-of-print. https://doi.org/10.1108/IJMCE-02-2021-0036.

Maslow, A. (1973), 'Theory of human motivation'. In: Lowry, R. J. (Ed.), *Dominance, Self-Esteem, Self-Actualization: Germinal Papers of A. H. Maslow*. Brooks/Cole, Pacific Grove.

Ofsted (2020), *Effective Mentoring and a Well-Paced Curriculum Are Key to High Quality Initial Teacher Education*. UK: Ofsted. Available at: https://www.gov.uk/government/news/effective-mentoring-and-a-well-paced-curriculum-are-key-to-high-quality-initial-teacher-education (Accessed: 28.04.2023).

Pierce, K. (2021), *Is Mentoring the Key to a Successful Career in Teaching?* Available at: Is Mentoring the Key to a Successful Career in Teaching? | Leeds Beckett University.

Roberts, A. (2010), 'Mentoring Revisited: A phenomenological Reading of the Literature', 8 2000 (2), pp. 145–70. https://www.tandfonline.com/doi/abs/10.1080/713685524

Thomson, B. (2013), *Non-Directive Coaching: Attitudes, Approaches and Applications*. St. Albans: Critical Publishing.

Van Nieuwerburgh, C. (2017), *An Introduction to Coaching Skills: A Practical Guide*, 2nd edn. London: SAGE.

Vare, P., Dillon, J., Oberholzer, L. and Butler, C. (2021), UCET Discussion Paper: Continued Professional Development, UCET Working Group, January 2021, UCET.

Wathen, N. (2021), 'High challenge and high support: A reflection on mentoring within a collaborative culture'. Available at: https://www.leedsbeckett.ac.uk/blogs/carnegie-education/2021/03/high-challenge-and-high-support/.

Whitmore, J. (2017), *Coaching for Performance*. London: Brealey.

2

Mentoring and Coaching Initial Teacher Trainees

Derek Boyle and Lizana Oberholzer

Aims and Objectives

The aim of this chapter is to give an overview of the processes involved in mentoring, and then coaching, a trainee teacher effectively. Trainee teachers are the lifeblood of the profession. They bring fresh perspectives and approaches to the existing teams within our schools, and they help mentors to engage critically with the latest research and ideas, which helps mentors and others supporting them on their journey to invigorate their teaching. Effective mentoring and coaching will enable trainees to become resilient career teachers.

This chapter will explore:

- Setting the initial expectations and ground rules of a productive mentoring relationship in place,
- Supporting the trainee teacher to establish themselves within their placement schools.

Introduction

Whether a trainee teacher has come straight from university or is a career changer, their introduction to the world of teaching and teacher training is going to be pivotal to their future success. It is important to add that the initial teacher training year is just that, 'initial', which means that this is the starting point of a lifelong commitment to professional learning, and it is the mentor's role to take the new teacher by the hand to guide them through this important first phase of their career. Teacher trainees don't evolve into 'readymade' finished products when they gain qualified teacher status; every year in teaching will be a continuation of the learning journey that they will start to embark on in these initial phases.

There are many different routes into teacher training, and these will all place their own expectations and demands on the trainee, mentor, training placement and the loved ones of the trainee. Although the Education White Paper (2022) might also bring additional changes to teacher education, the authors aim to capture the core principles of mentoring and coaching in ITT in this chapter which can be transferred successfully across different courses and pathways.

For ease of nomenclature, those undertaking the Initial Teacher Training (ITT) or Initial Teacher Education (ITE) will be referred to as a trainee teacher, although within their route and training institution they will be referred to by many different terms; in essence, all these routes are designed to train them to be a teacher.

If you are privileged to be given the oversight and care of a teacher trainee, your role as the mentor is a critical one in their future success and requires a great deal of thought and reflection. You will need to consider carefully how you need to, in collaboration with the training provider, shape the learning journey of the trainee as an adult learner.

The trainee will be relying on you to help them navigate the school culture, the ethos of the department or year team that they will be working within, the processes and procedures within the school, and to understand the politics within the organization they are training within.

Mentoring a trainee teacher requires self-reflection on your part, sacrifice of time and autonomy and a willingness to give of yourself to help develop the professional practice of another. These altruistic traits mark out a great mentor, along with humility and patience. We discussed in Chapter 1 what the national standards for ITT mentors and their roles are (DfE, 2016). We also started to explore how mentors and coaches need to consider developing relationships of trust from the outset of the learning journey.

Making Expectations Clear

The trainee teacher will have expectations placed upon them by the training provider, and it is important that you understand and plan for the workload implications that these will place upon the trainee. Trainees often engage with two or more placements in their teacher training year if they are engaged with a postgraduate qualification, but this might vary if they engage with an alternative pathway and more placements might be undertaken. The first step is for a mentor to plan a suitable induction for the teacher trainee with the ITT coordinator, and the activities outlined in Chapter 1 will be useful to draw on to develop a strong learning relationship with the trainee. Mentors are required to develop a suitable timetable for the learning phase the trainee is at, to ensure that they are engaging with the appropriate learning opportunities and experiences to help them develop and grow in line with the requirements of their course.

As the placement progresses the trainee will be expected to increase the number of hours of observation, collaborative teaching and whole class teaching. The expectations placed on them and the school by their training provider may be at odds with what is practicable for the team that you work within, but remember that the trainee has not dictated these requirements. The expectations placed on all members of your team by the training provider need to be translated and explained to the trainee as part of their induction. The new requirements by the DfE (2021) Market Review will also have more prescribed guidance on mentee engagements as well as requirements for mentors, which you will need to take into account when you plan for your mentee. Teaching and learning expectations, assessment procedures, recording and reporting processes and the culture and ethos of the school will need to be explained and, most importantly, modelled as well.

Modelling, similar to teachers modelling in the classroom to demonstrate to learners what is required of them, plays a significant role in teacher training too, and the National Mentor Standards (2016) highlight the importance of modelling too. Ratcliff-Daffron and Caffarella (2021) emphasize the importance of learning transfer and the application of learning for adult learners. Ibarra (2016) presents a model of outsight that advocates how adult learners need to evaluate their initial practice with their theoretical learning to develop, through their reflections, a deep understanding of the underpinning 'why' of their practice. Door (2014) stresses the importance of developing reflexive practices as educators to ensure that development and learning have a sustained impact in the behaviours that are required to make a significant impact over time. It is therefore important for the mentor to help the trainee not only to reflect on the protocols, practices and procedures but to understand what underpins their practice, why it is important and how it can make a difference.

Regular timetabled meetings between you and the trainee are going to be the most efficient way to monitor whether the expectations placed upon the trainee by their training provider, their team and their school are clear to them.

Evaluating the Needs of Your Mentee

For the duration of the time that the trainee is with you, they are your mentee, and your relationship is built upon clear and effective communication. Covey and Merrill (2010) stress the importance of continuing to build a trusting relationship. The importance of this relationship cannot be underestimated. Though the mentoring relationship is complex, it is important to uphold ethical standards, such as confidentiality, to ensure that this relationship is maintained, and it is imperative that mentors empathize and lead the mentee with kindness and compassion (EMCC, 2021).

From the moment that your new trainee steps into your school, you are going to be their touchstone who helps them to navigate the social, professional and political realities of being a new teacher in training. Even once they have qualified, you will remain a key influence on their outlook and their personal ethos of what it means to be a teacher.

The specific development needs of each trainee are unique, but they generally fall into the following categories:

- Phase/subject knowledge for teaching,
- General pedagogy,
- Phase/subject-specific pedagogy,
- Developing the confidence to talk to the whole class,
- Understanding their own response to challenges,
- How to deal with setbacks.

How the trainee develops confidence, and later competence, in each of these areas will be a combination of the central training element within their programme, the expected training that the placement gives them as well as their reading, research and reflection during their placement.

Within the first meeting with your trainee, you will need to provide an introduction and orientation to the working environment that they will be operating within. This goes further than introducing them to the rest of the immediate team that they will be working with and going through policies and procedures. They will need to understand the ethos of the team, the wider school and the nature of interactions with and between pupils through what is exemplified in the classroom, as well as gain a sense of what makes the school unique.

During the first few weeks, encourage your trainee to undertake a pupil pursuit, sit in and observe lessons with as many teachers that are within their own team and within other teams as possible, as well as to meet with senior leaders within the school. The meeting with the senior leader will help them to consolidate what it means to be a teacher within this specific school and serve to introduce the leadership role those senior leaders have. The notice senior leaders take of and investment that senior leaders make in the trainees within their school will have a major influence on whether the trainee will want to apply for a job at their placement school. If the trainee feels noticed and valued, they will more easily 'buy in' to the ethos of the school and become a brand ambassador for the school.

Once they have a sense of the school environment in which they will be operating, ask them how the school can help them to develop as a teacher against the six bullet points above.

Understanding Their Internal Challenges

When your trainee first steps in front of their first class, they will be feeling an overwhelming mix of emotions, but the strongest one is self-doubt. No matter how much planning and preparation they have undertaken and time they have put into fine-tuning their resources to cover all sorts of actual or perceived needs from the pupils, they will be too hard on themselves.

The feedback that you give them on their first few lessons that they teach will be crucial to their self-esteem and sense of self as a teacher. This will need some detailed planning from yourself and time to reflect, so make sure you have agreed a specific time and place for the feedback. The key with the feedback you provide will be that it needs to be carefully measured in line with the development phase of your trainee as discussed in Chapter 1 when we explored the Dreyfus Model (2004). Too much feedback might impact negatively on their confidence. Making sure that feedback is balanced with praise and specific areas for development will be key to helping the trainee layer their learning and build on their confidence.

Task

For each of these opening questions, think about what is said by the questioner, or mentor, and what is inferred by the mentee.

'When you were preparing for your lesson, did you read the school's assessment policy?'

This question opens with implicit criticism as it draws the initial point to their preparation and then that their use of assessment was 'not good enough'. As the mentor, did you go through how the assessment policy is used to support pupil progress?

'Reflecting on the lesson that you have just taught, what thing would you keep the same and tell me about one change that you would like to make if you were going to teach it again?'

The question infers that the lesson had good features, but it is also inviting the trainee to reflect on just one thing that they feel they could improve. This limits the trainee from explaining all the things that they perceived that has gone wrong.

Think about the opening questions that you use when giving feedback to your trainee. What are you saying to them through the message you are conveying?

When giving feedback, think about the implicit and explicit messages that you are giving the trainee through the way in which the feedback is delivered. Rushed feedback focusing only on what they need to do better in the next lesson over a cup of coffee in a busy staffroom is not going to help the trainee to rationalize what they have done well and the steps to success that they should address in their preparation for the next lesson. Being in a busy staffroom also compromises the need for confidentiality and a safe learning environment for engaging in learning conversations and creating the trust required of a mentor to ensure that the mentee feels safe, as outlined by Maslow (1943 as cited in Cameron and Green, 2020). Only when your mentee feels safe will they be able to open up to learning and to their personal self-actualisation as is outlined by Maslow.

The mentoring conversation that you will be having with them is just that: a conversation.

Think about the opening question that you are going to use and what message it is going to be sent to them.

The Importance of Empathy

When working with trainees it is important to remember that they are starting out on the journey of being a teacher. Try putting yourselves in their shoes. They are learning the professional habits and professional expectations of a new industry. You need to help the trainees understand what is achievable within the working week.

The trainee will look to you for inspiration and guidance about how to deal with disappointment and frustration, both with their classes and their colleagues. You need to agree with the trainee on what you can do and what you cannot do to help them on their journey of becoming a teacher. These ground rules will help them to navigate these professional expectations and new professional relationships while maintaining a sensible work-life balance for both you and the trainee.

As discussed in Chapter 1, you will find that as your mentee develops in their confidence, they will start to work towards independence and start to move away from requiring your nurturing advice, as described by Clutterbuck and Lane (2005). You will start to move on the continuum of coaching and mentoring (Buck, 2020), and you will find that, as the mentor or coach, you need to be listening more than you are saying. You will also need to be picking up on what is not being said, the non-verbal signals as well as the inference from their tone and general demeanour.

Setting Targets and Goals

When working with trainee teachers, the quality of the reflection and development as teachers is intrinsically linked to the quality of the targets that they are given and how they are encouraged to reflect on them.

Through giving them specific, highly focused targets, a trainee can build a professional framework of competence, like the way in which children develop schema (Rumelhart, 1980) to make sense of the work around themselves, but only through the social interaction of reflecting on their progress against those targets with their mentor.

This social interaction starts as self-reflection in a written form and then goes on to be discussed with their mentor, but this must be reinforced with a specific call to action through a SMART target.

As a reminder, a SMART target has the following components:

- **S** – specific, significant, stretching,
- **M** – measurable, meaningful, motivational,
- **A** – agreed upon, attainable, achievable, acceptable, action-oriented,
- **R** – realistic, relevant, reasonable, rewarding, results-oriented,
- **T** – time-based, time-bound, timely, tangible, trackable.

A poorly written and unfocused target from a mentor can lead to confusion and anxiety within the trainee, which will impede their development. For example, consider the following target:

'In order for your year 8 class to make better progress, focus on your behaviour for learning techniques during the transition between tasks.'

At first inspection, this target has a focus, *'better progress'*, and a way in which to achieve this is suggested: *'focus on your behaviour for learning techniques during the transition between tasks'*. However, what is meant by 'better progress'? When does it need to be achieved by?

Constructing this target using the SMART framework provides the following building blocks for the mentor:

- Specific – with your year 8 class,
- Measurable – reduce the amount of off-topic discussion on task transition,
- Achievable – through using the school's behaviour expectations, such as '3, 2, 1, eyes on me',
- Reasonable – so that you reduce the amount of time that you are waiting for the class to bring their attention back to you,
- Time-bound – before your next coaching observation.

The whole target would then become:

'With your year 8 class, reduce the amount of off-topic discussion on task transition through using the school's behaviour expectations, such as "3, 2, 1, eyes on me", so that you reduce the amount of time that you are waiting for the class to bring their attention back to you before your next observation.'

This then gives the trainee explicit guidance on what must be done, by when and using which strategy.

Depending on the training provider, you may then need to link this specific target to a specific sub-standard, but this can be considered good practice regardless of the provider's requirements as it will enable deeper reflection and enable the trainee to conceptualize how their learning is linked more clearly to their practice.

> **Task**
>
> Try rewriting these targets so that they are SMART-er.
>
> - Your year 10 books need to be marked on time and with comments.
> - Try and get involved with whole-school events with your year 3 teaching team.
> - For the upcoming Romans topic with year 2, help out with the planning and resourcing.

If we use the approach outlined by Clutterbuck and Lane (2005), the mentor should not just consider 'what' of the target setting process but also 'how' the mentee will be able to demonstrate an enhanced confidence in their practice that has been identified in the target setting process. Without thought as to the type of support that the mentee will require and consideration of any barriers to success that will need to be overcome, the process of improvement is going to be limited. Once the 'what' and the 'how' are considered in the target setting process, the discussion as to 'why' the target has been agreed therefore becomes the focus, because this then leads to a visualisation as to the form that success will take and how the mentee will recognize this.

Leading the Mentor/Coaching Meeting

When preparing for a mentor or coaching meeting, you need to walk into that meeting with a sense of what you want the session outcome to be. Good planning will enable you to get your trainee from where they are now to where they need to be in the short term and to where you would like them to be in the longer term.

Planning what you want to achieve in the meeting and what they must achieve as a result of the meeting is key to a developmental mentoring relationship. Framing this within the context of what they want to achieve and what they must achieve is a difficult balancing act.

> ### Task
>
> For your next meeting with your mentee, consider your responses to the following questions:
>
> - What is the purpose of the meeting?
> - What must you achieve by the end of the meeting?
> - What would you like to achieve by the end of the meeting?
> - What provision or resourcing will these require?
> - What will success look like to you?
> - What will success look like to the mentee?

Developing a Reflective Practitioner

For a trainee to develop as a reflective practitioner, they should be encouraged and given time to develop their own personal reflection on where their practice is currently and where it needs to develop.

According to Tice (2004), the most successful reflective teachers:

- Use existing knowledge to help develop their understanding of new ideas,
- Understand new concepts by relating them to their previous experience,
- Use additional research and reading to improve understanding,
- Critically evaluate experiences in order to develop their learning and thinking,
- Demonstrate self-awareness – they identify, evaluate and explain their strengths and weaknesses and identify ways to address them.

As the mentor, the way in which you approach your questioning, and the mentoring role generally, should be through encouraging mentees to reflect on their practices (Schon, 1983) and action plan for the next steps in the development of their teaching.

Your training provider may have a specific framework through which they encourage a process of self-reflection, but the trainee should be reflecting on the impact on their thinking of critical incidents in their experience either observing, co-teaching or teaching during a specific period of time.

A critical incident is one where the experiential framework that the trainee has built up during their training is challenged through what they have witnessed in a professional environment (Tripp, 2012). This could be in their own teaching or when observing another professional where the modelled behaviours have deviated from what was expected.

This reflection on their experience during the critical incident and then discussing it with their mentor gives a rich opportunity for the trainee to build a logical response and professional- or competence-based schema, which they can draw upon to respond to future critical incidents.

Observations and Feedback

When working with trainee teachers, their training providers will have their own unique and individual approaches to the collection of evidence in accordance with the Teachers' Standards (DfE, 2012). It is imperative that you understand and that you can explain those requirements to your trainee, as well as to colleagues and senior leaders. It is also important to share the trainee's specific targets to ensure that observations are focused rather than general in their approach. The training provider will have planned dates for training and briefing in school mentors, so you should seek these out to enable the placement to run smoothly.

Different training providers and different routes into teaching will have specific expectations put on their trainees and the school-based mentor that you need to be familiar with. The frequency and record keeping concerning coaching and formal lesson observation can cause anxiety for trainees and yourself as the placement mentor.

You need to be clear in your understanding of the purpose of lesson observation and how verbal and written feedback needs to be used by the trainee in the collection of evidence to show competence against the Teachers' Standards (DfE, 2012).

As a trainee teacher progresses through their placement, their confidence and competence will rise and fall as they start to work with different classes and ability groups across the school. You will need to ensure that a broad and balanced placement experience enables you as the mentor to help them develop as a well-rounded professional.

When framing feedback after an observation, remember that trainees will instinctively look for the negatives in their own view over their teaching. Avoid questions such as 'How do you think the lesson went?' Avoid asking the trainee to make judgements on their work; instead, encourage greater reflection. Try opening the feedback by asking them about how they feel the class made progress within the lesson, focusing on what specific pupils gained in terms of subject knowledge development and application as a result of the teaching that the trainee did. Alternatively, you can ask the trainee to talk you through the lesson plan, to frame the conversation and reflect on how each learning episode helped learners to progress. In this way, you focus on the choices and planning rather than the individual, so that the learning conversation becomes less threatening, and a safe learning environment is created.

You could ask them, if they were going to do that lesson again, what would they keep the same and what would they change. This implies that there are good elements within the lesson that they should keep and build upon and some things that they have the competence to adjust.

Transforming a Negative into a Positive – The Main Thing is Learning/ Developing a Positive Mindset

When working with new or relatively inexperienced trainees, a worry for new mentors is how to open the discussion around a poor lesson observation. It is important that the trainee and the discussion move quickly from what has gone 'wrong' to how things can be different next time. Avoid sharing an overwhelming amount of negatives, as negative bias can impact greatly on the trainee's progress and their confidence (Grenville-Cleave, 2016). Opening with a value judgement on the lesson can be destructive to the feeling of self-worth that the trainee has with their practice and shut down any further self-reflection and learning.

If you start the feedback with a question such as 'How do you think that went?', it can generally elicit two types of response:

- Self-critical – trainee focuses on everything that went wrong,
- Self-delusional – trainee does not recognize the shortcomings or development points in their practice.

One approach that can be used is to focus the opening questions on the experience of the pupils in the class and how the trainee thinks that they coped with the work that they were asked to do during the lesson. This approach forces the trainee to start from the point of view of the 'consumer': in essence, focusing on the pupil and not on their personal introspection.

Examples of opening questions could be:

- 'Whose work are you most pleased with today?'
- 'Who are you going to follow-up with next lesson?'
- 'Who do you think needs some further help in the next lesson?'
- 'Who do you know made the most progress today and why?'

Through getting the trainee to focus on the learning of the pupil(s) and away from their 'performance', the feedback session can then drill down into the most important aspect of the lesson, which is the learning and progress of the pupils.

Once the initial opening questions have been explored, start probing into the evidence that the trainee has for that view. This could then be pointing them towards the tangible evidence that you picked up during the observation, such as the work in the books or verbal responses from specific pupils.

By not making a specific value judgement on the effort that the trainee puts into any aspect of the planning, resourcing or teaching of the lesson, you are not enabling them to feel either defeated or defensive.

The Use of Positive Psychology

Within the mentoring relationship that you have with your trainee, the importance of the phrasing of questions and feedback is important to their development of an internal framework of self-belief that they can be a competent teacher. Their own self-belief that they can be confident as well as competent in this new role is built through the small incremental improvements, or marginal gains, that they make through each piece of feedback.

Try and communicate a belief in the trainee that, despite any setbacks that they feel or perceive, they are on a journey of development as a practitioner, and self-discovery and reflection are as important as the outcomes for the pupil. This use of positive psychology will help them to overcome the innate self-doubt, or imposter syndrome, that many teachers feel, particularly when training.

When we consider the well-being of trainees, the PERMA model, proposed by Seligman (2012), can be used to determine if adjustments need to be made in a mentor's practice or if the trainee is in a good state of mind for learning. The PERMA model states that well-being can be defined as a construct which includes the following aspects:

- Positive emotion
- Engagement
- Positive relationships
- Meaning
- Accomplishment

Someone who experiences high PERMA is considered to be in the optimal state of well-being, and they can be considered to be flourishing.

The positive relationships, both within the school environment and within their support network, are therefore important if we want the trainee to flourish. Developing these positive relationships is going to be based on their contributions and efforts being recognized and that they feel part of a bigger, collective community. The sense of meaning is the feeling that you belong to something greater or serve something which you believe is bigger than yourself, such as the school community or the ideal of a holistic education for all.

In the paper 'Teacher Well-Being: Its Effects on Teaching Practice and Student Learning' (Turner and Theilking, 2019), the authors highlight from their literature review the four strategies that align with PERMA research and contribute to optimal well-being in the working environment:

1. Use of character strengths of the individual to support the whole,
2. Social support which addresses engagement, relationships, and accomplishment,
3. Work-related attitudes, specifically how the individual finds their work meaningful,
4. Focusing on the positive aspects of one's work.

Translating this into the mentoring of trainees, we should strive to find the ways in which the trainee can contribute to the community of practice within their placement school and what positive contribution they can make. Supporting their development through using positive comments, tightly focused developmental targets and emphasising the positive contribution that they can make as new entrants to the teaching profession will help with their sense of well-being and accomplishment.

This needs to be tempered in helping the trainee to understand that your development as a teacher never ends and that each new pupil and each new class brings fresh professional opportunities.

Moving from Dependence to Independence

Over the course of the training placement with you, your trainee will develop in confidence, and then competence, with aspects of their teaching. These may be with specific year groups or specific subjects within primary. If you contextualize mentoring with a teacher-student relationship and a coaching relationship with working alongside someone to further develop their practice once they have reached a level of competence, you will see that this change in their behaviour will come. When you are happy that the trainee has developed confidence and competence in an aspect of their practice, your questioning with the trainee needs to move from a form of direct teaching and explaining to more exploring how they believe they can develop their practice further and deeper.

Through your coaching you are helping your trainee to become more independent in their thinking and approach to reflecting on their own practice. This can be supported through encouraging your trainee to read widely and to bring their own ideas to meeting a specific challenge that they feel that they want to overcome.

Promoting independence will help your trainee to flourish professionally and to enable them to feel as if they are becoming a valued member of the local professional learning community within your school or team. This then will allow the trainee to bring added value to the whole team through being able to participate in discussions and development work around the strategic development of the wider team and school. A fresh set of eyes on challenges and opportunities facing your school unhindered by convention is a valuable resource.

The added value that this brings to your team should not be underestimated as the experience they have within your team will heavily influence whether they apply for any Newly Qualified Teacher (NQT) roles within your school. The investment that you make in the trainee within your team will also have a wider impact on how the whole of the trainee body that the trainee belongs to views your school.

Facilitating Their Thinking

As part of the holistic development of trainees, they should be encouraged to undertake work on the bigger, holistic issues in education. These can be framed through enquiry questions which are linked to specific standards but are not linked to immediate short-term targets identified in self-review and the following target-setting and improvement cycle.

There is no single definition of enquiry-based learning; however, enquiry-based learning can be described as learning that arises through a structured process of enquiry within a supportive environment designed to promote collaborative and active engagement with problems and issues (Kahn and O'Rourke, 2004). Learning becomes more effective when students are actively involved in the learning process. Key characteristics of enquiry-based learning, according to Kahn and O'Rourke, are:

- 'Engagement – with a complex problem or scenario – that is sufficiently open-ended to allow a variety of responses or solutions.
- Students direct the lines of enquiry and the methods employed.
- The enquiry requires students to draw on existing knowledge and to identify their required learning needs.
- Tasks stimulate curiosity in the students, encouraging them to actively explore and seek out new evidence.
- Responsibility falls to the student for analysing and presenting that evidence in appropriate ways and in support of their own response to the problem.'

Within enquiry-based learning approaches, learners are encouraged to take responsibility for seeking evidence and analysing their knowledge for the purpose of making implicit reasoning and tacit knowledge explicit.

The authors propose a model that could be used to develop critically reflective practice in the trainee that is an adaptation of the spiral of enquiry model proposed by Bruner (1965) and the GROW model proposed by Whitmore (2017).

In this model the mentor and mentee would start at the explore stage with an identification of the centrality of the aspect of practice that is the focus of the enquiry.

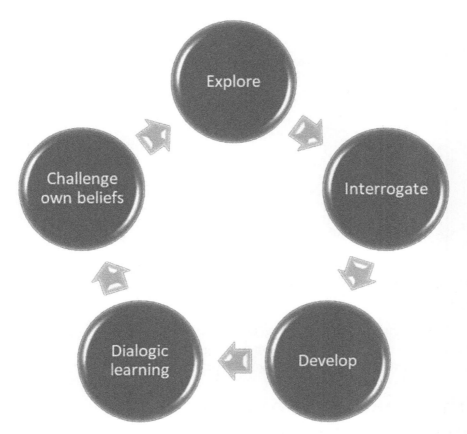

Figure 2.1 A model that could be used to develop critically reflective practice: An adaption of the spiral of enquiry model proposed by Bruner (1965) and the GROW model proposed by Whitmore (2017).

The interrogation of the founding assumptions that the enquiry question is based upon is the focus of this next stage. This is where the contributing factors that could be explored as part of the enquiry are identified and discussed. Prioritisation of the relative perceived potential impact that these factors could have on the outcome of the enquiry question is established.

Next, the mentee develops a plan of action based on how the potentially most impactful factors can be investigated and tested.

The dialogic learning phase is where the plan of action is interrogated by the mentor and mentee with a series of 'what' and 'how' questions that leads to an understanding of 'why' the exploration of this enquiry question is important for the development of the practice of the mentee.

The next stage is where the mentee is encouraged to challenge their own beliefs that underpin the course of action using probing questions to help consolidate the course of action into defined actions.

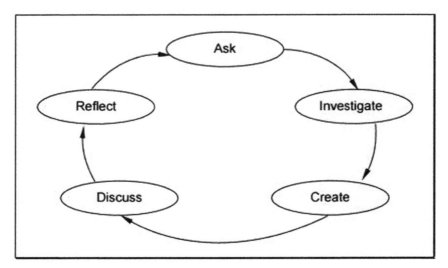

Figure 2.2 Encouraging your trainee to engage with self-initiated enquiry by Bruner (1965).

Encouraging your trainee to engage with self-initiated enquiry will help them to see self-development and their own learning as a holistic continual development process and not a series of skills to show competence in and move on from.

The Importance of Reflecting on Well-Being When You Train to Teach

When working with trainee teachers, you are helping them to develop their confidence and competence against the Teachers' Standards (DfE, 2012), but equally as important, you are helping them to adjust to and build stamina for the realities of being a 'career teacher'.

Teaching needs to be seen as a vocation and a lifestyle choice for those entering the profession, so you are helping them to adjust to this reality while they are training.

As the placement mentor, you need to be cognizant and considerate of the explicit and implicit workload that the trainee is under. Within the Bromley Schools' Collegiate School Centred Initial Teacher Training (SCITT) course for example, it is explained to the trainees that they should be planning for the total working hours as a trainee to be around fifty hours per week, as they are training for a career as a teacher, and this is the reality of the profession that they are entering.

When you meet with your trainee, ask them what they do to relax and how they are going to keep 'down time' within their week. It is important for their own well-being that they keep time aside every day and every week to maintain social and familial contact with their loved ones and for hobbies.

When working with your trainee, consider what sort of example you set for them. How do you maintain a healthy work-life balance? How can you help them navigate the personal and professional relationships within the school environment in a positive and developmental way? How can you help them to be integrated into the team and the wider school family?

Trainees come into their Initial Teacher Training through a variety of routes and come from a myriad of diverse backgrounds, so try not to assume that someone coming into teaching from another profession is 'better' at handling the reality of being a teacher than someone straight from university. Their lived experiences and ability to cope with change are not a function of age alone.

> ## Task
>
> Ask your trainee to complete a timetable for themselves running from 6:00 am to 10:00 pm Monday through to Sunday and then fill in the times that they are travelling to and from school, when they are on site and any specific intervals each week they are in central training.
>
> Then ask them to fill out when they will be eating and spending time with family each day, as well as time they will be planning, resourcing and marking work. Within the week, ask them to fill out time that they will be spending on themselves. This could be listening to music when walking the dog, going to the gym, reading, carrying out a hobby or participating in a sport.
>
> Once they have completed this timetable, ask them to put in weekly reminders for themselves when they have specific fixed deadlines for their training programme or their placement school, such as resource requests or weekly reflective documents.

If they have childcare responsibilities, you need to be aware of them as their mentor. These need to be handled sensitively and practically as the arrangements for dropping them off prior to coming into the placement school can be majorly impacted by travel delays and congestion. When a trainee is already late in the morning because of traffic or a last-minute loss of childcare, the last thing that they will need is a lecture from their mentor. Helping them to navigate how they can handle this type of situation within a professional environment is where your experience will be valuable.

Finally, think about how you are going to help the trainee to integrate into your existing team, as being the only trainee within an existing team is a daunting prospect. Including them in tea rotas, secret Santa and the planning for World Book Day can help them to embed them into the team.

Training to teach is just one aspect of their life that they are having to manage, and you can think of it as a single plate they are continuing to spin along with all of the other aspects of their life.

Case Study

The following case study was written by Mary Davis, an ITT mentor, and it shows the importance of allowing the trainee teacher to have the space to grow and develop their professional practice within a supportive and nurturing environment.

During my career, I have been privileged to mentor trainee Geography teachers. This is something I am passionate about. I think it is vital that our new teachers feel supported within their training year and are able to build the necessary skills and mindset to carry out their roles effectively and sustainably.

I particularly enjoy supporting the student teachers through their first year, which is, inevitably, a challenging one as I am able to see them grow, build resilience and develop within their career.

Being a mentor involves scheduled weekly meetings as well as informal meetings when required by the students or for observations, setting targets and encouraging the students to reflect on their practice.

One impact of mentoring is allowing the trainee teachers the opportunity to reflect effectively on their teaching practice. It is important to build up trust with my mentees to ensure they feel comfortable in reflecting on their own practice. Mentoring gives the students the space to reflect truthfully without judgement, which leads to positive changes, having built the confidence to analyse their teaching practice.

Another impact of mentoring is giving the student teachers the opportunity to feel empowered within their own personal development. Through mentoring, I am able to share my experiences within the profession and impart my knowledge. But it is important that, as the mentee moves along their journey, they continue to work on their continuing professional development in order to ensure they are able to enhance their strengths and continue to develop in their roles.

As well as encouraging my mentees to reflect on their experiences, the processes inspired me to continue to reflect on my own practice. Having the opportunity to work with student teachers with fresh innovative ideas motivates me to try new teaching and learning strategies, which I am then able to reflect upon. Through mentoring I became more informed and enhanced my own expertise.

As part of the mentoring process, I hoped to have played a role in producing teachers who are able to build relationships with students, reflect on their practice and understand how they can improve and build on each of their lessons. Furthermore, it is important to me that my mentees feel valued within the profession as this enables them to feel confident in embracing any challenges they may face.

Within my role as a mentor, I intended to ignite a passion for my subject and education as a profession. I aimed to give my mentees the confidence to feel they can voice their contributions and strive for improvements within education beyond their classroom. Trainee teachers play a vital role as the next generation of teachers in education to inspire our young people and promote sustainable education.

Moving forward I aim to take the skills I have learnt through mentoring trainee teachers and mentor members of my team in order to support them to further develop within their roles. While my team all hold different roles, I believe that through effective mentoring, you can show team members what they are capable of achieving in their individual role, in turn enhancing their ambition, which, of course, will improve the overall performance of the team.

Reflective Task

1 After reading this chapter, how are you going to ensure that the welfare and well-being of your trainee teacher is at the centre of your mentoring relationship?
2 In your mentoring meetings, how can you ensure that the focus of the meeting is solely on their development? How are you going to ensure that external disruptions are kept to a minimum?
3 In the case study, Mary explained the impact that being the mentor has had on her. What are your motivations for becoming an ITT mentor?

References

Bruner, J. S. (1965), 'The Growth of Mind', *American Psychologist*, 20(12), pp. 1007–1017. https://doi.org/10.1037/h0023276.

Buck, A. (2020), *The BASIC Coaching Method: All You Need to Know to Coach with Confidence*. UK: Cadogan Press.

Cameron, E. and Green, M. (2019), *Making Sense of Change Management: A Complete Guide to the Models, Tools, and Techniques of Organisational Change*, 5th edn. London: Kogan Page.

Cameron, E. and Green, M. (2020), *Making Sense of Change Management: A Complete Guide to the Models, Tools, and Techniques of Organisational Change*, 5th edn. London: Kogan Page.

Clutterbuck, D. and Lane, G. (2005), *Situational Mentoring: An International Review of Competences and Capabilities in Mentoring*. UK: Sage.

Covey, M. R and Merrill, R. R. (2010), *The Speed of Trust: The One Thing That Changes Everything*. UK: Simon & Schuster.

DfE (2012), *Teachers Standards*. Stationer Office. London.

EMCC (2021), *Global Code of Ethics*. UK: EMCC. Available at: Global_Code_of_Ethics_EN_v3.pdf (emccuk.org) Accessed: 28.04.2023.

Grenville-Cleave, B. (2016), *Positive Psychology: A Toolkit for Happiness, Purpose and Well-Being*. UK: Icon Books Ltd.

Ibarra, H. (2016), *Act Like a Leader Think Like a Leader*. USA: HBR Press.

Kahn, P. and O'Rourke, K. (2004), *Understanding Enquiry-Based Learning, Handbook of Enquiry & Problem Based Learning*. In Barrett, T., Mac Labhrainn, I. and Fallon, H. (Eds.), Galway: CELT.

Ratcliff Daffron, S. and Caffarella, R. S. (2021), *Planning Programmes for Adult Learners: A Practical Guide*. USA: Jossey-Bass.

Rumelhart, D. E. (1980), *Schemata: The Building Blocks of Cognition*. UK: Routledge.

Schon, D. (1983), *The Reflective Practitioner*. London: Temple Smith.

Tice, J. (2004), *Reflective Teaching: Exploring Classroom Practice*. India: Support Foundation.

Tripp, D. (2012), *Critical Incidents in Teaching: Developing Professional Judgement*. London; New York: Routledge Falmer.

Turner, K. and Theilking, M. (2019), 'Teacher Wellbeing: Its Effects on Teaching Practice and Student Learning', *Issues in Educational Research*, 29(3), pp. 938–60. Available at: https://search.ebscohost.com/login.aspx?direct=true&db=eue&AN=138293232&site=eds-live (Accessed: 4 December 2019).

Whitmore, J. (2017), *Coaching for Performance*. London: Brealey.

Recommended Reading

Cope, Andrew N. (2019), 'Flourishing in the workplace: An investigation into the intentional strategies employed by those experiencing long-term positive affect in the UK public sector'. figshare. Thesis. https://hdl.handle.net/2134/27375.

Oberholzer, L. (2020), *Why Mentoring and Coaching Matters When Starting as a Teacher Trainee*, CollectivEd [12], pages 56–58, Carnegie School of Education, Leeds Beckett University.

3

Mentoring and Coaching Newly Qualified Teachers and Early Careers Teachers

Lizana Oberholzer and Derek Boyle

In this chapter the authors aim to help you:

- To develop a clear understanding of how to reflect on the needs of Early Careers Teachers (ECTs) to meet their needs as professional learners
- To consider how mentoring and coaching need to be utilized to provide the learning support required for ECTs to enable them to flourish.

Introduction

Concerns regarding teacher retention and the recruitment of new teachers are not new concerns. Moor et al. (2005) highlighted that, at the time, the profession lost more than a quarter of its newly trained teachers within the first five years. Since 2010, the profession had seen unimaginable changes and reforms, as well as workload increases, which are often cited as one of the biggest reasons for teachers leaving the profession. The Teacher Wellbeing Index (2021) also highlight that teacher workload is a key concern. However, in the authors' own research, NQTs, or as they are now referred to as ECTs, often highlight that behaviour is one of the biggest concerns for them, followed by teaching and learning practices, understanding how to support learners with different learning needs and Special Education Needs and Disabilities (SEND), as well as, when they are teaching in a secondary school context, how to support learners on their post-16 journey, in relation the ECT's subject specific expertise.

In an attempt to address the teacher retention concerns, the Department for Education (DfE) published the department's retention strategy in 2019 as well as the Early Careers Framework. The Early Careers Framework sets out to provide development opportunities for teachers in the early stages of their career across the two years following their initial teacher training year. The Early Careers Framework stimulated a wide range of debates, and there are key criticisms regarding the prescriptive nature of this framework. However, it is also a welcome opportunity to offer support, guidance and a two-year support plan for teachers, which are fully funded. It is not a new initiative, and it is important to recognize that prior to the 2010 education reforms, Training Schools led on Early Professional Development (EPD), with funding grants, and had differentiated teacher standards in place for all phases of a teacher's development provided by the Teacher Development Agency (TDA), as well as fully developed programmes. This support was removed due to the new reforms and was replaced by Teaching Schools, and a single set of Teachers' Standards (DfE, 2012), which are now further developed in the ITT Core Framework, ECF framework and National Professional Qualification (NPQ). In the spirit of this book, the authors aim to focus on how mentors and coaches can work positively within these various frameworks to make the most of the opportunities for NQTs, and Early Careers Teachers (ECTs) to enable them to grow. Moving forward the acronym ECT will be used as an umbrella term to refer to NQTs and new teachers engaging in their learning for the first two years of their careers as teachers.

Referring to mentoring from the outset of this chapter, and in the chapter title, is a deliberate choice, as the authors aim to set out, how ECTs need to make a transition into their new teaching role either within their existing context or within their new teaching context. The Early Careers Framework (ECF) (2019, p. 4) states that teachers in the early stages of their careers need 'high quality' support in a supportive and 'structured' way and that teachers need to 'develop the knowledge, practices and working habits that set them up for a fulfilling and successful career in teaching'. The ECF provides teachers in England with a fully funded, structured programme to engage with for two years to ensure that they are able to develop the knowledge, practices and habits that lead to a long, impactful and fulfilling career. However, the ECF, though making reference to mentors and the support they can provide through the suggestions in the 'Learn how to ...' statements on possible mentoring that can be received, does not outline how mentors need to develop to ensure that they support professional learners to make the transition from their training year into their new roles. It is important to reflect on how mentors need to develop and shape their own learning to support those in their care. The authors argue that it is a key part of the successful rollout of the ECF to consider how mentors need to be developed, to develop their own learning and understanding of where the ECT is at and to enable them to meet the learning needs of the ECT fully on this learning journey.

Bleach (2016) reflected on an Ofsted report in his work and outlined that ECT support varies greatly from context to context. Similar to Initial Teacher Training (ITT) practices, as outlined in the Carter Review (2015), Bleach states that during the ECT year, the learning, development and mentoring often do not continue to build on the ITT experiences of the ECT. The ECF's (2019) 'Learn how to …' statements remind of the Teachers' Standards (DfE, 2012) and key points that ECTs and mentors need to explore on the journey. However, it is key that mentors develop their own clear understanding of where the ECT is at, and what the ECT's specific needs are, to ensure that the ECT can make a strong transition into their new role and context. Bleach (2016, p. 3) points out that if the transition between the ITT year and the ECT year is not carefully considered, 'slippage' can take place where the ECT adapts to the dominant practices and ethos of the school they are in within weeks of their placement, regardless of the value and currency of the learning and training they had during their ITT year. This might also be why some Early Careers Teachers (ECTs) often make the assertions that they did not learn much during their ITT year and that most of their learning took place during their teaching or with their mentor.

Supporting adult learners needs to be considered in a variety of different ways, and often, being exposed to an initial theory might not quite make sense at the time or until the ITT or ECT experienced the situation, and they are able to look back and make sense of the situation by reflecting in and on practice (Ibarra, 2015; Schon, 1983). Door (2015) stresses the importance of the mentor's role in these in-depth discussions and reflections and points out that the mentor needs to help facilitate the sense-making (Weick, 1995), through the exploration of the 'why', and the research and theory that underpins possible choices that the ECT made and what the learning points are. The mentor's role is also to help the ECT to explore, more deeply, what underpins their practice and how different theories, research and perspectives need to be considered within the framework of the context they are working within.

The process is complex and nuanced, and the mentor's own understanding of mentoring needs to be in depth in relation to how the ECT will need to be supported on the journey. In addition, the mentor will need to have a strong personal subject base and understanding of the pedagogical practices within their own disciplines and the phases that they teach. Mentors need to continue to engage with mentor development beyond their understanding of engaging with the ECT and what the 'Learn that …' and 'Learn how to …' statements set out in the framework. The authors argue that it is a good starting point but should not be seen as a 'tick box' exercise; the mentor and mentee need to be creative within these structured frames to unpack the journey fully.

Mentoring an ECT

When starting the ECT learning journey with your mentee, the authors recommend that you revisit some of the points made in Chapter 1 regarding the development phases of the mentoring relationship as well as the skills development phases that need to be considered for ECTs as discussed in Chapter 1.

It is often important to remember that ECTs completed their ITT year as teacher trainees and that they qualified as initial trainees. Their assessments reflect their performance appropriate for the phases where they were at in line with the Teachers' Standards (DfE, 2012) as teacher trainees. They have the skills required for the initial phrase; however, the ECT phase aims to progress and deepen the ECT's learning journey. There are often criticisms, by ECTs and others in the teaching profession, that as ECTs, they felt they still had so much to learn. The irony is that the professional learning journey is continuous and continuing, and the initial phase is just that; it is the starting point to a long journey of learning. ECTs cannot possibly be the finished product compared to colleagues with thirty years' experience as classroom practitioners. School leaders and mentors need to be clear on the fact that ITT courses provide a strong foundation to build on, but the ECT's learning needs to continue as they become more confident and progress through their own career.

In many ways, the ITT year is a compact and intense learning experience of nine to ten months, and a vast amount of content is covered in that time. The learner's capacity to retain it all is unlikely, but the seeds are sown to provide a foundation that will enable the learner to return to certain points when needed. At times in the ITT year, based on the authors' experiences in leading ITT courses, learners might not encounter opportunities to work with learning assistants or go on a trip or work with learners with specific learning needs; this might only happen during the ECT year. Their ITT year might be filled with rich experiences of working with learners with English as an Additional Language, or very gifted learners, ECTs' experiences can vary.

Although the content was covered regarding these important topics in the initial teacher training stage, the consolidation and putting-into-practice stage still needs to happen during the ECT phase. The honest truth is that teaching is a cumulative process, heavily set within the contexts that teachers work in, and often the professional learners' journey only centre around a certain focus when they are encountering it at that point in time. Before then, they will have a broad understanding of the issues. The reality is that all teachers are continuous works in progress, and that is also why it is such a rewarding profession where we continue to learn as collaborative professionals within our learning communities.

At times, from the authors' own experiences working with ITTs and ECTs, these new professionals place a high premium on executing their work to perfection, and these behaviours become more pronounced in a system of high challenge and high stakes (Myatt, 2016). However, the authors argue that schools and mentors need to have a realistic take on where the mentee is at as a newly qualified teacher and that ITT does not and should not create ready-made teachers. We should instead continue to invest in shaping the development opportunities and learning curriculum for the ECT that enables them to grow and extend their learning appropriately for this phase of their journey.

The question is often also, what is appropriate? What should be included in the learning diet for an ECT to ensure that they flourish? The ECF provides an outline of the entitled learning within the ECT's learning framework. However, similar to ITTs, ECTs might all be on different learning trajectories, and some will be able to confidently step into their new role as a newly qualified teacher and others will need to be taken by the hand more. Some ECTs might even take on leadership roles at this stage, depending on the school's circumstances they work in, and their prior experiences in other contexts, as career changers. It is the mentor's role to initially be clear on where the mentee is at on this learning journey to ensure that they consider how they will work with them to provide the appropriate support. The mentor needs to understand how much guidance and support are needed or if the ECT needs a different approach such as coaching. Too much guidance for a more experienced, confident ECT might have a negative impact on their autonomy and motivation (Pink, 2018), or too little support and guidance for a less confident NQT might cause them to feel unsafe and insecure on their learning journey (Maslow, 1973).

Introductions

When meeting your ECT for the first time, regardless of whether they are new to your context or not, always remember that they are progressing to the next phase of their learning journey. Within that new phase they are often in the novice phase of their skills acquisition (Dreyfus, 2004). For some, this novice phrase might take a while to work through, and for others it might only be a short while to progress to an advanced beginner phase or a proficient ECT phase. Most schools provide an induction event, which can be a day of induction or a week with a detailed programme, and, as Bleach (2016) points out, practices vary. However, make sure that you are also well prepared for your ECT's arrival, even if they are your previous ITT student, celebrate this next step and make them feel welcome. Teachers so often forget how important it is to celebrate their successes, and building on the positive is key, as the journey for ECTs, like ITTs, are often challenging in the initial stages. The first 6 weeks of starting a new role can be the most challenging.

It is often helpful, if it is a new colleague you have not mentored before, to share with them the pre-meeting questionnaire:

1. Introduce yourself to your mentor by providing a brief summary of your learning journey so far (100 words).
2. Reflect on your ITT year; what were the key highlights during that year?
3. What are your personal interests?
4. What do you hope to gain from this year?
5. What do you feel are your strengths in relation to your subject knowledge?
6. What do you feel you want to continue to work on?
7. What are you hoping to gain from your mentor?
8. How do you hope to engage with your mentor?
9. What questions do you want to ask your mentor at this stage?
10. In 100 words describe the teacher you are hoping to develop into.
11. What are you looking forward to during your first ETC year?
12. What is your favourite book?
13. What are your hobbies?
14. What else do you want to share with your mentor?

Similar to the induction for ITTs, you might also want to ask for a summative Curriculum Vitae and their final ITT report, and in some contexts, they often also provide a 'transition point' document, which will provide you with a clear outline of the needs of your ECT and next targets.

Often these targets are fairly broad or written directly after the ITT assessment, and the ECT might have continued to teach and work in schools since the time of writing the report. It is therefore important to review the report and its content with the ECT to see if the targets are still relevant and whether they need to be refined more, to allow the ECT to make a good start during the year. The Final ITT Report is often written with the Teachers' Standards (DfE, 2012) in mind or the ITT Core Framework, which will provide a helpful needs audit for the ECT, and it will be useful to go through the document, too, to be clear on whether the targets for the different documents align, whether they are still appropriate or whether new targets need to be set to start the first week off positively.

Talking through the ECT framework is also helpful, and the document with the various statements in line with the Teachers' Standards is a helpful document to start off with to enable the ECT to highlight any potential gaps.

In the first two weeks of the ECT's journey, it might be worth agreeing a supportive lesson observation to help you see where they are at in relation to their planning, teaching as well as behaviour management, and you can discuss this as a possible initial first step with them in your initial meeting. The key is to highlight that it is a supportive observation, that you will not take notes and that it will not be used for any assessments. The authors often explain this to professional learners by comparing this to a teacher's review of a learner's previous learning to enable them to plan effectively, and this conversation often helps to create that safe learning space needed by learners to develop a relationship of trust with you as a mentor (Buck, 2020; Covey, 2006).

During the induction, have a handout or pack ready for the ECT containing their timetable; class lists; data, including learner needs data; department/ phase handbook; assessment dates; medium-term plans; and any other resources they might need. It is often helpful to provide them with some board pens, rubbers and information regarding the photocopier, resource office and any key staff they need to be aware of from the outset. By having this ready, they will start to make sense of the new context and their new role.

Your first meeting is key, when considering Clutterbuck and Lane's (2005) model, to build rapport and trust. Having the above ready in preparation for the meeting will make all the difference and will enable you to move onto your learning conversations more quickly. Having regular mentor meeting slots already slotted into the timetable will also help cement the ways of working with the mentee.

Making Expectations Clear

It is also helpful in the first conversation to outline the expectations in relation to how you want your ECT to engage with the mentor meeting. Making the expectations and boundaries clear is a necessary step to ensure that the ECT can start well.

Outline the following:

- When will meetings take place?
- What does the ECT need to bring with them to the meeting?
- What preparation does the ECT need to do to engage effectively in the meeting?
- How are meetings conducted?
- Where do meetings take place?

As mentor, make sure that you are also considering where the meeting takes place carefully. It is often unhelpful to engage with meetings where ECTs need to share confidential issues with you in the staffroom. Make sure that you book an appropriate meeting room to enable your mentee to engage fully with the meeting. Make sure that you respect the confidential nature of the relationship too, and do not discuss the ECT's progress with peers in the staffroom. It seems obvious to say this, but it does happen, and it is difficult for the ECT to continue to engage with the mentoring relationship in a trusting way moving forward once they discover that their data is shared with others without consent.

When engaging with the ECT make sure that you enable them to discuss their learning and ensure that you reduce the amount of talking on your end to enable the ECT to share and reflect on their practice throughout. You will find that the initial conversations might reflect a 40 per cent or 60 per cent ratio of the ECT sharing and discussions versus the mentor providing guidance and advice. However, once the relationship is becoming more established, there will be an emphasis shift to a 70 per cent or 30 per cent, where the ECT will reflect and share the most compared to your role as mentor becoming a facilitation role, framing and managing the conversation.

Leading Mentor Meetings

Leading an effective mentor meeting is essential; it is a good way not only to encourage deep reflection but also to model good practice where the mentor and the mentee make the most of the time available for the meeting. It is often helpful to ask the mentee to draw up an agenda prior to the meeting that outlines what they are hoping to discuss during the meeting to ensure that the meeting is focused. In the authors' experience having a framework, like an agenda, is helpful as it keeps both the mentee and mentor on track, and the mentee can email it to you prior to the meeting to enable you to add key points too. In addition, having an agenda in advance will enable you to plan how you might want to frame the learning conversation and provides you with an opportunity to consider what resources to bring with you prior to the meeting. It is often good to remind yourself of what the previous targets for the ECT were to help frame the start of the meeting. It is good practice to keep short summaries of the meetings and to share it with the mentee, or if you want the mentee to take ownership of this, they can email a summary to you after the meeting to agree. If you work in a large team, and your mentee also work with a range of colleagues who support in joint planning or other team activities, you can also ask your mentee to share the relevant targets with colleagues via a weekly summative email after the mentor meeting.

Meeting agendas can have standing items on them, for example, reviewing the previous week's targets and reflecting on your main achievements for this week. It outlines what the next points are to consider.

The meeting summaries can include the following headings or questions:

1. Reflection on previous targets – are there any targets that we need to consider further?
2. What reading and research did you do to help you to meet these targets?
3. How do these targets align with the Teachers' Standards and ECF (2019)?

4 What are the next steps?
5 How do these steps align with the Teachers' Standards and ECF (2019)?
6 What resources do I need?
7 Who do I need to talk to?
8 What do I need to read?
9 Do I need to observe anyone to see how it is done?
10 What are next week's targets?
11 What time frame do I have to complete my targets in?
12 What was my main learning point that my mentor discussed with me?

Note how the headings tend to include what, how and who questions.

At the start of the mentor relationship make sure that you create a safe learning space, and by drawing on 'what', 'how' and 'who' questions, you will tend to enable the conversation to open up as a learning conversation. At times 'why' can lead to defensiveness, and it is often best to move into 'why' much later on in the learning conversation to ensure that you strengthen the learner's confidence and ability to reflect first (Thomson, 2013). As you can see, in the headings and planning, the mentor encourages reflection by asking questions around the relevant reading and the learner's engagement in driving their own learning journey. However, this also allows for further discussions on recommended reading and opportunities for learners to ask questions they might have regarding their own work. There is a cycle of reflection built into the framework, and the key is to enable the mentee to reflect and draw on their learning and identify where they are becoming stuck, to offer potential guidance or solutions.

MacIntyre and Hagger (1992), as cited in Williams (1993, p. 412), outline that there are different levels of mentoring. Bleach (2016) reflects on this dynamic in his work, too, and the levels of mentoring are outlined as follows:

Table 3.1 Levels of mentoring an adaptation from Bleach (2016)

Zero	Generic expertise, not aligned to the specific needs of the ECT.
Minimal	Practical guidance which includes, strategies to plan, strategies to manage classrooms and behaviour effectively, and organizational policies and approaches.
Development	Acknowledges the complexity and nuanced challenges teachers face when supporting learners and the learning process, and exploring approaches to work in collaboration with others, in communities of practice.

However, the authors want to adapt this model even further by reflecting Door's (2015) point that mentors need to ensure that they offer opportunities for reflection within their mentoring conversations with their mentees to ensure that they progress and move forward.

Table 3.2 Levels of mentoring including opportunities for reflection an adaptation from Bleach (2016)

Some mentor support	Involves very general professional expertise not specifically related to the needs of new teachers. A light touch approach, where mentor meetings do not take place regularly.
Minimal mentor support	Offers practical support in areas like planning skills, classroom practice and information about the school's organisation. Mentoring centres around practical aspects and ways of doing rather than deepening the mentee's understanding of the underpinnings of practice.
Developmental level	Recognizes the learning process is complex and becomes involved with strategies like collaborative teaching. Enables the mentee to have a clear understanding of how key theories and research need to be considered within their practice, and mentors help facilitate the thinking during mentoring meetings to enable the mentee to explore why key choices are made as part of a research informed approach to their practice. A wide range of research and perspectives are considered in a reflective way to inform practice fully.

Development Challenges for NQTs

It is important for mentors to enable their mentees to engage with their own learning on a deep level. Mentors also need to have a clear understanding of the development phases of mentees to lead the mentor meeting well. In Chapter 1, the Dreyfus Model (Dreyfus, 2004) was explored in relation to the skills acquisition of the mentee, and the mentor needs to continue to evaluate where the ECT is at in relation to their development to adapt their mentoring support to meet the learner's needs consistently. Understanding where the ECT is at is key to a successful mentor relationship. Maynard and Furlong (1995) explored the professional growth and development phases of teacher trainees, and the authors argue that similar patterns are often noticed when mentoring ECTs and adapted the original model proposed by the Maynard and Furlong as follows:

Figure 3.1 Maynard and Furlong's (1995) model of professional growth and development phases of teacher trainees.

As a mentor, make sure you have a clear understanding of where your mentee is at. When they are new to a school or a role, they often have an idealistic view of what needs to happen. When situations become challenging, they are often disillusioned by their experience. At this stage of their career, as a novice, make sure that you support and guide them to help them develop a growth mindset approach to their learning (Dweck, 2010). In this way they will be more willing to take risks and develop their thinking to grow into their role with more confidence. Once they developed strategies to cope with the new challenges and start to explore the challenges they face with you, you might find that they slip into patterns of working and hit a plateau in relation to their growth. This means that you might often see the same lesson plan being used, or worksheets used, opposed to planning mirroring the needs of the learners the ECT needs to support. You will find that your ECT's lessons plans for all year groups follow the same formula, for example, or they might become over-reliant on worksheets.

This is where you can challenge a bit more by asking questions in relation to what they can explore, read, engage with and try out. When you do challenge, make sure that it is at a manageable level, where they take small incremental steps to try out, for example, different strategies to question or where they embed one new activity or strategy within the lesson. Help them to cement this first before moving onto the next step.

A helpful approach at this stage might be to identify key research to look at with your mentee, for example, on behaviour management. There are many resources available, offering curated pieces that you can look at and frameworks to use to help you facilitate the learning of your mentee. We recommend one such book below in this chapter; however, the Chartered College of Teaching offers a fantastic resource on its website for ECTs, which you can draw on too. Work through the piece with your mentee, identify two to three strategies they might want to draw on, identify a colleague they can observe who uses similar strategies to see how the theory translates into practice. It is often useful, if you do have the time, to observe with the mentee to point out where the strategies are used. If not, meet afterwards and discuss their key learning using some of the questions already discussed in the meeting summary framework. Collaboratively plan how the new learning will be used in the next lesson, and collaboratively teach the lesson to see how the new learning can be embedded in the NQT's practice.

Observation and Feedback

Observations are a key part of the teacher trainee's learning journey during their ITT year. During the ECT year, ECTs are observed regularly too; however, not as often as they would do during the ITT year, unless the mentor or Senior leader for CPD feels that there is a key need to support the NQT further on their journey. The authors want to stress, as they have done from the Introduction of the book all the way through the various chapters, that mentoring and coaching should not be aligned with such high stakes support, as it often is. When learning is engaged with in this way, through observations, the key is for it to be predominantly formative and supportive.

For example, in the previous section, we discussed how a mentor can support a ECT after setting a specific development target focusing on behaviour management. The aim was to illustrate how developmental mentoring can facilitate the learning journey, and as part of the journey, an observation can follow in a formative way where the focus of the learning is explored and what the next steps need to be to continue to learn. The main thing needs to be learning (Hughes, 2003).

Facilitating Thinking during Feedback

A helpful strategy to draw on is to use the mentee's own thinking to explore the lesson plan more fully and the thinking behind the lesson plan. Often mentors start with 'how do you think it went?' This a tricky question, as you need to remember that being observed heightens the ECT's limbic system. They are already in a stressed state, and the first step after an observation is to ensure that the ECT is feeling safe. Asking 'how do you think it went?' requires of the ECT to make a judgement on their own performance. At times, the lesson did not go so well, but it is important to reassure the mentee that these are the best learning opportunities, and this is where truly helpful learning conversations can take place. The mentor and ECT can then enter into a useful learning conversation once the ECT is calmer and more settled.

A technique to help build on the reflections and thinking for the mentee is to use the lesson plan they developed for the lesson. Ask the mentee to talk you through the lesson plan, rather than you just sharing your written feedback. It is a bucket effect when you just deliver your thoughts; whereas asking the mentee to reflect helps them to unpack what worked well, where the issues were in the lesson, what decisions were made based on their previous learning, how the lesson unfolded and what the next steps need to be to refine their practice even more. By using the lesson plan as a focal point, rather than the performance, and by discussing the choices and how these impacted on the learning, the focus is on the pupils' learning. In this way, you move away from a deeply personal onslaught for the mentee to a more reflective thinking approach where open questions are used, and they can learn to make sense of their own learning more effectively.

Setting Targets and Goals

Based on the reflections and learning shared during the discussion around the lesson observation and lesson plan, the next step for the mentor and ECT is to identify new targets. Helpful questions to ask are:

- Based on our conversation regarding the lesson and the lessons plan, what are the five key things to consider when looking back?

- If you had to narrow it down, what are the two most important things to focus on for your next lesson?
- How do you feel you can achieve this?
- What resources do you need?
- Who do you need to talk to about this?
- What reading do you need to do regarding the current research around this focus?
- Who do you need to consider to observe?
- How do you aim to embed your learning into your practice?
- When will you be ready to share this part of your learning with me?

When to Coach and When to Mentor

In the above examples shared, the authors model how some mentoring and coaching strategies overlap, and of course, the questions asked in the above section mirror that of more open coaching questions to start moving the mentee into the driving seat, to become more independent on their learning journey. In Chapter 1, the authors discussed the importance of making sure that you meet the needs of the mentee. It is important here to progress to a coaching approach in an appropriate and a transparent way, as outlined in Chapter 1, but at the right time for the mentee. It is imperative to ensure that the mentee moved past the novice and advanced beginner stage to ensure that they are able to reflect on the questions you ask more confidently. Moving on to a coaching approach too early might impact on the ECT's confidence and a more gradual approach might be more helpful.

Drawing on Coaching Strategies to Support Mentees

Both mentoring and coaching require of the facilitator of learning to listen actively, ask good questions and engage with the professional learner in a trusting and supportive way. During learning conversations, one of the key techniques to use is playing back what was shared, summarising the learning. Often ECTs will think out loud, and by playing it back to them, you check that you heard correctly and demonstrate that you did listen carefully, and they often hear their thinking in this way for the first time, which can often lead to great insights. Listening is a key part of mentoring and coaching, and it makes the ECT feel safe and feel they are being supported as well as valued. However, it is a fantastic tool to help develop thinking and learning – as the active listening and paraphrasing, playing back and getting summaries help the learners to think through their practice more carefully (Thomson, 2013).

The Importance of Reflection

During collaborative learning conversations and reflections, ECTs continue to learn the value of deep reflection in and on practice. By co-teaching and planning, ECTs are able to see how you model your practice and how you make the choices you make based on your research and how you consider key points in practice (Schon, 1983; Door, 2015). By engaging with your ECT in a supportive way through your learning conversations, they will get a detailed and clear understanding of how they need to plan, and teach, as well as reflect in their practice as well as in the learning conversations afterwards that look back and reflect on their practice. Developmental mentoring, at this deep level, will provide the ECT with a strong foundation of not only the effective teaching practices in place but an in-depth understanding of why those choices were made in line with the relevant research they engaged with as well. Discussing teaching, learning and theories is key, as Knapper (2000) and Mezirow (1991) remind us that theory influences practice, and that practice impacts on how theory is developed. How we conduct ourselves in our practice also impacts our thinking. It is therefore important to be aware of the fact that learning occurs when we are engaged in the action, as well as looking back on the action.

The role of the school senior CPD Lead or, as referred to in some schools, the professional mentor and ITT co-ordinator cannot be underestimated in their support of the mentor's role. For example, Yamina is a professional mentor in an inner-city school in London who leads the induction and the support for ECTs in her school. She describes in the following case study the way in which she supports her colleagues:

> As a professional mentor, I believe that effective mentoring is the difference between success and failure for Early Career Teachers (ECTs). To support ECTs in our organisation, mentoring the mentors has been integral to support ECTs to thrive. This included providing internal training for all mentors to know how to give effective feedback to their mentees. To support ECTs, I created standardized agenda items which outlined specific pedagogy and pedagogy content knowledge to focus on and deliberately practice in weekly mentor meetings. Additionally, each NQT has an E-File where they evidence meeting the Teachers' Standards, write weekly reflections on lessons and write reviews on current reading.
>
> As a result of the standardized agenda items with a focus on deliberate practice, ECTs have been able to spend time with their mentors honing their practice before implementing them in the classroom. Mentors feel more confident as a result of the regular training and are able to identify specific action steps for their mentees. These conversations in mentor meetings alongside the deliberate practice have led to mentors being able to identify

the next steps for their mentees, and there has been clear improvements in classroom practice of Early Career Teachers. As ECTs develop their practice, mentors have moved from providing targets and action steps towards a more coaching approach. This has meant that mentees choose their next steps from a range of options, so they feel empowered in their classrooms.

As part of the school's focus on developing teacher expertise and excellence, we are hoping to continue refining the mentoring programme for both mentors and ECTs as this is integral to their success. This will include a focus on instructional coaching to ensure that trainees receive bitesize, practicable and observable action steps weekly to help continually develop their pedagogy. We hope to continue supporting mentors in this role by providing regular training during directed time as a key part of the role.

Yamina's case study reflects how an agenda can help shape the learning conversations during mentor or coaching conversations effectively. She outlines how these agenda points linked to a specific focus can help to focus the conversations and empower both the mentor or coach and their NQT. There is a clear emphasis shift to a coaching approach where the NQT can reflect more deeply on their learning and next steps. Reflection is at the heart of the support outlines, and Yamina outlines the importance of small incremental steps throughout the learning journey too, as discussed earlier on in the chapter.

Reflective Task

- What are your three main learning points after working through this chapter?
- How will you consider the development phases of your NQT when you support them as a mentor or coach in future?
- What strategies can you draw on to help shape your mentor conversations and mentor summaries in future?

Recommended Reading

Chartered College of Teaching (2020), *The Early Careers Framework Handbook*, UK: Corwin Ltd.

Capel, S. Lawrence, J. Leask, M. and Yournie, S. (2019), *Surviving and Thriving in the Secondary School: The NQT's Essential Companion*, UK: Routledge.

Chartered College of Teaching (2021), 'The Early Career Hub'. Available at: The Early Career Hub – The Chartered College of Teaching's Hub for Early Career Teachers (Accessed: 01.06.2021).

Robinson, C., Bingle, B. and Howard, C. (2020), *Surviving and Thriving as a Primary NQT*. UK: Critical Publishing.

A book providing mentors and mentees with curated reading and research to reflect on behaviour management challenges in the classroom, as well as helpful reflective tools, and frameworks to support mentors and NQTs on their journey:

Oberholzer, L. (2019), *Behaviour Management: The Essentials*. UK: Routledge.

References

Bleach, K. (2016), *The Introduction and Mentoring of Newly Qualified Teachers: A New Deal for Teachers*. UK: David Fulton Publishers.

Buck, A. (2020), *The BASIC Coaching Method: All You Need to Know to Coach with Confidence*. UK: Cadogan Press.

Covey, S.M.R. (2006), *The Speed of Trust: The One Thing That Changes Everything*. UK: Simon & Schuster.

Department for Education (2012), *Teacher's Standards*, UK: DfE. Available at: https://www.gov.uk/government/publications/teachers-standards (Accessed: 01.06.2021).

Department for Education (2015), 'Carter review of initial teacher training'. Available at: https://www.gov.uk/government/publications/carter-review-of-initial-teacher-training (Accessed: 01.06.2021).

Department for Education (2019), 'Early career framework: A framework of standards to help early career teachers succeed at the start of their careers'. Available at: Early career framework - GOV.UK (www.gov.uk) (Accessed: 01.06.2021).

Door, V. (2015), *Developing Creative and Critical Educational Practitioners*. UK: Critical Publishing.

Dreyfus, S. (2004), 'The Five-Stage Model of Adult Skill Acquisition'. *Bulletin of Science Technology & Society*, 24 (10), pp. 177–79.

Dweck, C. (2010), 'Mind-Sets and Equitable Education'. *Principal Leadership*, 10, pp. 26–9.

Education Support Partnership (2021), 'Teacher Wellbeing Index 2021' [WWW Document]. URL: https://www.educationsupport.org.uk/media/5pgbh1bn/twix_2021_3_mental_health_of_education_staff.pdf (Accessed: 04.01.2021).

Ibarra, H. (2015), *Act Like a Leader, Think Like a Leader*. United States: Harvard Business School.

Knapper, C. K. (2000), *Lifelong Learning in Higher Education*, 3rd edn. London: Kogan Page.

Lane, G. and Clutterbuck, D. (2005), *Situational Mentoring: An International Review of Competences and Capabilities in Mentoring*. UK: Sage.

Maslow, A.H. (1973), 'A theory of human motivation'. In Lowry, R. (Ed.), *Dominance, Self-Esteem, Self-Actualization: Germinal Papers of A.H. Maslow*. (pp. 153–73). Monterey, CA: Brooks/Cole Publishing. (Original work published 1943).

Maynard, T., Furlong (1995), 'Learning to teach and models of mentoring'. In: Kelly, T., Mayes, A. (Eds.), *Issues in Mentoring*. London: Routledge.

McIntyre, D., and Hagger, H. (1992), 'Professional Development through the Oxford Internship Model'. *British Journal of Educational Studies*, 40, pp. 264–83.

Mezirow, J. (1991), *Transformative Dimensions of Adult Learning*. UK: Jossey-Bass.

Moor, H., Halsey K., Jones, M., Martin, K., Stott, A., Celia, B., and Harland, J. (2005), *Professional Development for Teachers Early into Their Careers: An Evaluation of the Early Professional Development Pilot Scheme*. National Foundation for Educational Research.

Myatt, M. (2016), *High Challenge, Low Threat*. Woodbridge, UK: John Catt Educational Ltd.

Pink, D. (2018), *Drive: The Surprising Truth about What Motivates Us*. USA: Canongate Books Ltd.

Schon, D. (1983), *The Reflective Practitioner*. London: Temple Smith.

Thomson, B. (2013), *Non-Directive Coaching: Attitudes, Approaches and Applications*. St. Albans: Critical Publishing.

Williams, A. (1993), 'Teacher perception of their needs as mentors in the context of developing school based initial teacher education'. *British Education Research Journal*, 19(4), pp. 407–20.

Weick, K. (1995), *Sensemaking in Organisations*. London: Sage.

4

Mentoring and Coaching Recently Qualified Teachers/ Early Careers Teachers

Derek Boyle and Lizana Oberholzer

Aims and Objectives

This chapter will aim to examine how you can support the transition of a recently qualified teacher (RQT), which is a teacher progressing beyond their second year in teaching up to the fifth year of teaching. Early Careers Teachers (ECTs) will receive a detailed support plan for the first two years of their teaching journey; however, after the second year, the support will become less, and often at this point, RQTs will start to make the transition into leadership too. RQTs tend to receive a less regular method of mentoring which often transitions into coaching as explained in Chapter 1, when we explored the continuum of coaching and mentoring, and they might also take on new roles or engage with the newly introduced specialist National Professional Qualifications (NPQs), where they might receive coaching support as required by the provider delivering the course or in their schools, depending on how the NPQ is shaped. However, coaching is not a prescriptive requirement for these programmes, and support might vary. It is therefore important to reflect on how continuous support will be put in place for RQTs too, to continue to enable them to engage with their roles as teachers and future leaders.

The purpose of mentoring and coaching with recently qualified teachers change, and colleagues need to be able to adapt their practice accordingly, so we will be looking at:

- How to support RQTs with establishing themselves professionally within the school,

- How to help RQTs to develop their career aspirations,
- How to help RQTs to establish and maintain a realistic and healthy work-life balance.

Introduction

The mentoring of recently qualified teachers should be a central strand of the talent management and capacity building strategy of the school in which they work. Coalter (2018) highlights the importance for organisation to have a strategy in place to retain staff, to build capacity and to practice succession planning. These teachers will in future form the supportive and experienced teachers that the middle and senior leadership teams will be relying on to implement change, and to maintain teaching and learning standards within the school. This group of teachers are also the next generation of future leaders within the school. Retaining and developing these teachers will provide the strength in your teaching teams and providing high-quality mentoring and coaching should be seen by the school as an investment in these staff to retain them (Tomsett and Uttley, 2020). Coaching and mentoring practices need to become part of each teacher's development toolkit, opposed to it often being used for more sinister purposes and practices.

When you are assigned to be a mentor or coach for a recently qualified teacher, you need to establish what the needs are of the RQT and reflect on where the emphasis of your support needs to be:

- Is the focus of your mentoring and then coaching to develop them as better classroom practitioners, or is the aim to support them as future middle leaders?
- Do you aim to enable them to engage with wider school responsibilities and projects?

A helpful way to reflect on establishing the RQT's needs might be to create a SWOT (Strengths, Weaknesses, Opportunities and Threats) analysis with them. In your first mentoring or coaching conversation, you might want to reflect on what their strengths are, where the areas for refinement might be, what the possible opportunities might be that they can consider and what the potential challenges might be and how to work around these. A SWOT analysis is a simple tool to use, but it provides great insights into the needs of the colleague you aim to support. You might also want the RQT to reflect on what they would like to achieve within the next two or three years to give you a sense of their personal aspirations and goals. Blanchard et al. (2018) highlight that it is imperative to know what development stages your members of staff are at to enable you to determine when to coach and when to mentor. Remind yourself of the Dreyfus Model (Dreyfus, 2004) in Chapter 1 and where you think the RQT you are working with might be at on his or her learning journey and skills acquisitions to enable you to reflect on how you can meet their needs and reflect with them on how to move their journey forward.

Making Expectations Clear

Recently qualified teachers have less weekly support compared to their first two years as Early Careers Teachers (ECTs); however, the transition from being 'nearly' qualified to a recently qualified teacher could be made in over as little time as six weeks, depending on their circumstances.

> **Reflection Task**
>
> (*You might want to develop a reflective learning journal to explore the questions below*)
>
> - What are the parameters for the mentoring or coaching that you are undertaking?
> - Who has assigned you as a mentor or coach? What might the agenda be?
> - What must be achieved?
> - What would your line manager like the mentee to achieve?

When to Coach and When to Mentor

The approaches that you should take when working with recently qualified teachers depends upon whether they have been established within the school from when they qualified as a teacher or if they have moved at the completion of their induction. Some recently qualified teachers may have undertaken very substantial placements within their current school of employment and therefore might have three or four years of experience of working within the school ethos and culture already.

Mentors or coaches working with these teachers require an approach where they are developing and building upon the existing pedagogical capital and experience that RQTs have built up since joining the school, depending on their existing confidence and competence within the classroom and contributions they are making to their teaching team. When looking at the Dreyfus Model in Chapter 1, you will notice that the RQT you are working with might now be at competent or proficient stage, which means that a coaching approach might be more suited to what they need. Alternatively, you might be working with an RQT who just moved to your school, which means a mentoring approach might be suitable at the beginning stages of the journey as they are a novice to your school, but they are perhaps competent or proficient in their teaching, and as a result, will progress quicker through the skills acquisition phases to a point where you need to recontract the learning relationship and move on the continuum of mentoring and coaching to support them effectively as a coach (Buck, 2020). You may need to utilize either a coaching approach or a hybrid of a mentoring and coaching approaches, depending on your RQT's needs.

Buck (2020) and Thompson (2013) outline the coaching and mentoring continuum as follows:

Figure 4.1 Buck (2020) and Thompson's (2013) mentoring continuum.

When moving on the continuum of coaching and mentoring, the mentor would use a mentoring approach to support the development of newer skills and competences to extend and develop their existing experiential-based portfolio of skills, combined with a coaching approach for aspects of their role where they are showing high levels of competence. Striking the right balance between the aspects of this continuum will need to be developed on a case-by-case basis. For recently qualified teachers who have moved employment mentoring might be a more suitable approach as they have yet to adapt to the existing culture and ethos of the employing school that they will be joining. They will be bringing a wealth of contrasting experience with them from their previous employment, and as a mentor you should be looking at the way in which they can utilize their emerging expertise as an early career teacher to strengthen existing teams.

Your early meetings with these recently qualified teachers will require a mentoring approach initially until the range of experiences and competence that they bring with them is understood by the mentor. The identification of these emerging strengths will reveal themselves during the first year in the school and will require the mentor to nurture and develop a self-awareness of these strengths over time.

Supporting the RQT with Their Development Goals

Recently qualified teachers may well be in the first throws of enthusiasm for their developing career, and it is important to recognize and nurture these career development goals. The role of the mentor is to prompt and sustain the discussion with the early career teacher around where they see themselves in the next few years and what experiences they need to have in order to progress to this next stage in their career.

As the mentor you will also have an understanding of who has relevant experience within the school that can shape your mentees' understanding of the experience and skill set needed in order to progress to this next stage in their career. Your role then becomes one of facilitation and enabling the mentee to explore the agency that they will need to develop in order to make this next step in their career. Developing agency as well as unlocking the RQT's potential is a key part of supporting colleagues who are starting to progress further on their learning journey. Durrant (2019) highlights that developing agency in teachers is vital in addressing school improvement.

At the same time as you are helping to nurture the career aspirations of your mentee, you need to also help them to consolidate their classroom experience so that they can build up the pedagogical and experiential capital and be seen as a 'credible' candidate for promotion, either internally or in another school. In Chapter 1, Clutterbuck and Lane's (2005) model of the mentoring relationship was explored, and it was highlighted how the mentor relationship progresses towards a more independent stage where the mentee starts winding down the 'nurturing' aspect of the relationship. It might be at this point that you need to start recontracting the relationship to progress to a coaching approach to enable the RQT to start developing their independent approaches and practices and use the learning conversations to help them to make sense of their learning more effectively (Weick, 1995).

As a recently qualified teacher, your RQT will have spent their time and effort in consolidating their subject knowledge for teaching, pedagogical approaches and classroom teaching experience. Now they should be looking to fill gaps in their teaching experience with different year groups or a broader range of classes to enable them to develop their practice. This consolidation of classroom experience will be vital currency with which they can then push towards the next steps in their career.

During your learning conversations, start exploring with your RQT their own career aspirations and their motivations for progressing their career along these pathways. To help frame a discussion here are some prompt questions that you can use:

- What do you enjoy about your current role?
- What do you see as your next career development stage?
- What are the qualities and experiences that you feel that you need to have to take this next step?
- How can you develop the knowledge and skills to undertake this next step?
- What can I do as your mentor to help you gain this knowledge and experience?
- What do you feel that you can bring to a role such as this?

An approach that some schools use is the development of *leadership incubators* for staff who are identified as future leaders within the school, and this is where the mentor can play a vital role in facilitating the establishment of these. It is important to recognize that leadership in this context does not just mean a leadership role within a hierarchical structure but also an aspect of subject pedagogy or a cross-school aspect of the coordination of the work of staff. Enabling the RQT to have agency and see that they can make a profound impact on the learning of others is a very important next step for the RQT, to realize that they can lead and influence in a variety of different ways (Durrant, 2019).

One model that can be used is the use of action learning sets (Brockbank and Mcgill, 2003). Action learning sets can be used to help future leaders develop their understanding of leadership roles, school systems and practices. Action learning sets, as defined by (Brockban and Mcgill, 2003), is a process which involves small groups of people who use skilled questions to share issues and find solutions. By joining a leadership action learning set, future leaders can shadow existing leaders and also work with them to unpack possible issues and think of ways forward and possible solutions by using the action learning set reflection tool.

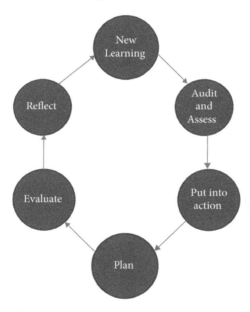

Figure 4.2 An adaptation of the action learning set reflection tool by Brockban and Mcgill (2003).

It is important to identify colleagues who will be suitable to shadow and join the action learning set to help develop the RQT as a future leader. This may require senior or middle leaders, mentors or coaches to identify suitable colleagues to engage with the process and to coordinate the group and bring them together. It is important for 'buy-in' that the parameters and purpose of the grouping is clearly communicated to the participants and that the purpose of the group is for mutual support to give them space to discuss professional challenges without any perceived threat or organizational hierarchy.

Action Learning Sets Normally Work as follows

Step 1: In the first five minutes of the conversation, previous learning or observations are explored. Success is celebrated and progress is reviewed.

Step 2: A presenter is selected; in this case it is often the more experienced leader, to share an issue that was observed during the shadowing done by the RQT of the Leader. The issue is explored for ten minutes, and the RQT and facilitator do not interrupt.

Step 3: The RQT and facilitator have an opportunity to ask questions regarding the issue shared (ten minutes).

Step 4: The leader shares their reflections by selecting two to three questions they found most useful and unpack how these questions helped them to consider how to move forward.

Step 5: The facilitator reviews the discussion and unpacks the key learning points by facilitating the thinking of the RQT and leader and agreeing on their next steps.

The facilitator's role within this leadership incubator is to provide the time and space for the meetings to occur and then to step back. The mentor or coach (at this stage the role will start to transition more strongly into coaching) is facilitating a talent management strategy and enabling the pipeline of future leaders within the school and profession where future leaders are nurtured via collaborative professional communities (Hargreaves and Rolls, 2021).

Useful questions to ask during the facilitation of the action learning set:

Good Questions to Ask for Clarification:

- What is currently happening?
- What is your perspective on this issue?
- What other issues do you need to consider?
- How does this issue make you feel?
- How does the issue make others feel?
- Who might help you?
- Who might be most affected? Who might be harmed?

Good Questions for Gentle Probing

- What is the difference between the current situation and the way you would like to lead the change?

- Who else do you need to involve?
- Can you give an example of *X*?
- Can you define who 'we' and 'they' are in your narrative?
- What assumption are you making?
- What are the barriers?

Good Questions to Facilitate Action

- If you had complete freedom to address the issue, what would you do?
- What are the potential options you can consider?
- What else do you need to consider?
- What research do you still need to do regarding the matter?
- What is your first step to move this issue forward?

Helping Your Mentee Become More Confident in the Classroom

As teachers we all aspire to improve our professional practice and retain that critically reflective approach that we were taught during our initial period of training that led to Qualified Teacher Status. Some recently qualified teachers can suffer from an over confidence in the quality of their teaching that maybe masking an inner turmoil, which can be rooted in a feeling that is similar to imposter syndrome. Browne (2020, p. 48) defines imposter syndrome as a belief or feeling that we are 'a fraud or a fake'. As the level of formal support that the RQT received as a trainee and early career teachers falls away, the professional learner can feel that they need to bottle up concerns and perceived weaknesses in their practice.

As the mentor, you will need to ensure that you establish a careful balance between professional accountability and facilitating an open dialogue where the mentee can express any lack of confidence in their own practice and seek guidance on how they can develop and deepen their own practice in a supportive environment. You will again need to make a judgement call on how you need to move on the continuum of coaching and mentoring to ensure that you support your professional learner effectively.

As your mentee gains and deepens their professional experience within their current school, your role as the mentor becomes one of supporting them to gain both confidence in their practice and competence in teaching across a range of different year groups. As they come towards the end of each year you should be considering where their next deployment within the school should be and discuss this with the member of the senior leadership team that timetables the staffing across the school.

Once you have discussed the options available to your mentee, prepare for a further developmental discussion with them.

The following prompt questions can help you to frame a developmental conversation with your mentee:

- Reflecting on your professional practice this year, what have been your specific successes?
- If you were going to start this year again with the same class(es), what would you do the same, and what would you do differently?
- Which of your learners are you most proud of and why?
- Where do you see your professional learning gaps?
- How could you address these gaps?

When using these questions, remember to use pauses and silence when they are giving their responses as a prompt for them to expand on their responses. In addition, use supplementary questions such as:

- Why do you think that?
- So, what was your main take away from that experience?

At the end of the session, reflect what they have said back to them by rephrasing their responses and asking if that is what they meant by the statement. This reflection and rephrasing process allows you to not only show that you have comprehended their responses but also gives them a chance to confirm their thoughts back to you.

At the end of the questions and reflection, open the discussion about the options for them in the coming year and discuss which of these options most closely meet the developmental aspirations that they have expressed.

Evolving Their Understanding of Effective Teaching and Learning

Throughout their Initial Teacher Training and their Induction period, your RQT will have been required and encouraged to critically engage with education research, but there is a tendency once the induction period has been completed for this to 'fall off the radar'. Competing demands on their time will inevitably result in the time and mental space for keeping abreast of educational research to be greatly reduced.

The risk the RQT faces is falling into a confirmatory loop, where the existing pedagogies that they utilize are seen to be successful, and they then rely upon a tool kit of approaches that fit a bias towards what feels comfortable and supports their current viewpoint or approach (Maynard and Furlong, 1995). To challenge this loop effect, your role as the facilitator is to help your RQT to re-engage with critical reflection on their own practice and then support them with being a critical consumer of educational research.

A strategy that you could explore with your RQT is through modelling this behaviour yourself first through bringing a piece of pertinent research to a mentoring session and sharing it with your mentee so that they can see how you have engaged with it and applied your own learning to your practice. An accessible approach that you could use with your mentee is sharing an article from the Chartered College of Teaching (https://chartered.college) or the Education Endowment Foundation (https://educationendowmentfoundation.org) that you have read and used yourself within your own teaching.

Here are some prompt questions to help you to prepare for modelling this process yourself:

- Explain the main points of the article or piece of research.
- Explain how you have used the ideas presented in your own teaching and why.
- Explain why the piece of research is applicable to your context within the school.

This process will model how you have used a critical approach to the selection and use of research within the context that you both find yourselves working in. The next stage is to ask your RQT to repeat the process for themselves utilising a piece of reading or research that they have found interesting and applicable to their context.

The three-step approach that you modelled can then be used by your mentee at your next meeting.

As a follow-up activity with your mentee, this can then be extended through asking your RQT to introduce a piece of relevant research at a future team meeting to share their learning with the wider team. You will need to help, support and advise your RQT with the preparation for this opportunity, as the first time that they share their professional learning with the rest of the team can be daunting.

A structure that could be used by your RQT to introduce and frame the piece of research is given below:

- What is the purpose of the research?
- What was the context of the research?
- What did the research conclude?
- How is the research applicable to our context?
- How did I apply this reading or research to my own practice?
- How could we apply their findings to the practice of the team?
- What would be the logical next steps for the team if they adopted this approach?

After the team meeting, spend time with your RQT to ask them to reflect on how they felt the presentation and discussion went to help them reflect on their own learning from the process. This will help them to internalize the learning process and provide support and encouragement to them to continue with this approach.

Working with the RQT on Developing Career Pathways

As your RQT deepens their understanding of their professional practice, they will naturally start to consider how they wish their future career to shape itself. Their professional instincts will start to shape themselves into a desire to progress towards either more curriculum focus or perhaps a more pastoral focus.

As their mentor or coach, you should start to design and engineer opportunities for them to find out more about the different career paths that exist within the school or trust that they are part of. From your conversations with your RQT, what are their career aspirations? What opportunities can you help to provide for them to explore these roles? Who do you know within the school organisation that you can provide the opportunity for your RQT to spend some time with and perhaps shadow them? Are there any opportunities within the school for your RQT to shadow an existing post-holder or to take up an acting, or assistant, role for a fixed period of time?

Providing structured opportunities for your RQT to explore these roles and then gaining their thoughts and reflections on the knowledge and skill set needed to be successful within that role will show the level of investment that you personally, and by extension the school, is making in their retention.

Starting to Explore Leadership Roles

When you are working with your RQT to start exploring leadership roles, there are a number of different activities that you may want to try with them to help them to develop a deeper understanding of the principles of leadership that they will need to have a grasp of when they take that next step up.

Contributing to Team Meetings

If you have a recently qualified teacher who is interested in developing and exploring leadership roles, providing opportunities for them to contribute to team meetings provides a safe environment for them to develop a leadership profile within the team. These initial leadership opportunities could be introducing a moderation exercise across the wider team or introducing them to a new resource or approach that has been seen to be successful.

When setting up this opportunity for your RQT, discuss with them in advance what the parameters of this opportunity are and ask them what they see success as. Ask your RQT to propose the way in which the activity will be led and then ask them to rehearse the range of responses to the activity that they might expect from the team. Rehearsing or role-playing responses to the activity from the personalities in the team is an important exercise for emerging leaders to work through to understand the needs of the team and also their response to turbulence and change.

Prompt questions:

- How will you define success for the activity that you will be leading?
- Who will be the biggest supporter in the meeting? And how can you harness this in the meeting?
- Who could provide opposition to the activity? What could be the reason for the opposition?
- How can you utilize their expertise to help make the activity a success?

Shadowing Line Management Meetings

As the mentor, you could introduce your RQT to the line management process by asking your own line manager if your RQT could join you for part of your own meeting. As an observer, this gives a chance for the mentee to understand the range of areas that are covered within a typical line management meeting. After the meeting, this gives you the chance to discuss their observations of the meeting and their reflections on what sort of preparation you would normally do in advance to be fully ready for the meeting.

This developmental process enables the mentee to understand the range of skills and strands that a leader needs to have at their fingertips at all times.

Developing an Understanding of the Needs of the Team

An exercise that can be used with RQTs is asking them to analyse the strengths and areas for development within the team in which they currently operate. It is important that you maintain an understanding with the RQT that their reflections and thoughts are treated confidentially and will not go any further, but they need to frame their thoughts within a professional approach, focused on observable facts, avoiding supposition and assumption.

For each member of the team, ask the mentee to consider the following prompt questions:

- What are their demonstrable strengths?
- How are they supporting the work of the team?
- What opportunities can be developed for them to grow as a professional?
- Where are their areas of development?
- What can the team do to support them with these areas for development?

Facilitating Thinking Time

Within the normal working week of most teachers, they are spinning a number of plates continuously, not only their own individual practice within the classroom but also within a number of simultaneous roles across the school. They will be managing a whole multitude of relationships with their pupils, the parents or carers of the pupils, immediate colleagues and with their own family, all of which require emotional stamina and resilience.

When we ask these busy professionals to then consider their own professional development, career aspirations and enhancing their professional knowledge, we can see that as mentors that this is just adding to their existing workload. We need to make the mental space for them to have downtime, where they can take a step back from their daily routines and multitude of roles that are calling on their time and mental bandwidth.

As the mentor, ring-fence time within each of the meetings you have with your mentee is an opportunity for your mentee to think and reflect. Meetings can easily be taken up with the minutiae of the grind of the operational aspects of being a teacher, so create the space for you both to take a pause. Within this ring-fenced time, ask your mentee about their career aspirations and which parts of their distinct roles they feel that they have been successful within. Use the time to show that you are invested in them as an individual and not just as a cog in the machine. Perhaps discuss an issue that is causing them a professional dilemma and ask what you can do to support them outside of the meeting and follow through with the support that you offer. When they know that you 'have their back', this will strengthen the relationship between you.

Case Study

The case study below, written by Sydney Porter, illustrates the critical role that a good quality and committed mentor can have on the development of recently qualified teachers. It is important to recognize the effect that this developmental process also has on the mentor and how these skills can then be translated into supporting other groups of staff as they progress their careers.

I first started using coaching and mentoring when I began supporting an NQT who was left without a mentor due to leadership changes during a very turbulent time at the school. Through the work I completed with this NQT, focusing on planning, behaviour management and teaching strategies, we focused a large portion of our time on English. We have continued this relationship over the past two years as she has progressed into an RQT and further in her career. I have now started to support aspiring middle leaders as they begin the climb into leadership.

The work I completed with the NQT provided her stability and support not only during a tumultuous time within the school setting but also in a critical point of her establishing herself as a teacher. While our relationship started with a heavy focus on mentoring, the following year we began to work along the continuum between coaching and mentoring, depending on the focus of each session. Through the relationship, the NQT was able to self-identify areas of improvement and set goals for her own practice, while it also enabled us to observe one another teaching, plan collaboratively and receive feedback. With many opportunities to work together, provide guidance and begin to interweave coaching questions into the relationship, often more than one goal was identified at any given time, which accelerated the progress the NQT made. With our relationship continuing into the following school year, and still part of our working relationship today two years later, this participant has told me one of the most significant impacts of our relationship is not only the positive impact on her confidence within the classroom but also as a practitioner within the wider school context. While our relationship initially started as a mentor-mentee one, we have moved to the coaching end of the continuum – often she is asking the questions of herself and is further developing her reflective skills on her own practice in supporting decisions she is making on a day-to-day basis.

In the past year, I have started to work with newly appointed middle leaders (ML) or those aspiring to middle leadership positions. I feel this is a vital area to provide support, particularly coaching, as this is an area that lacks adequate training opportunities. With the removal of the National Professional Qualification in Middle Leadership (NPQML) and the replacement by subject specific NPQs, the training on offer for ML has decreased further. By providing coaching and mentoring to those aspiring for leadership positions, not only are they receiving context specific experience but are also developing their understanding of the role while being supported in building their confidence to carry out the leadership tasks. Rather than being thrust into the positions with little to no training, as we see many ML have been in the past, providing tailored, one-to-one support will not only prepare them in their career progression but will inevitably bring consistency within the school context and ensure leadership standards remain highly functional, continuing to positively impact student performance.

Well-Being, Workload and Retention of Your RQT

When working with your mentee, remember that you should be mindful of their well-being and work-life balance as well as your own. Striking the right balance between providing the support that they need to flourish during their early career phase must be balanced with helping them to develop the resilience that is going to be needed to retain them in the teaching profession.

As your mentoring relationship is developed and sustained, you will be helping them to become a reflective teacher and guiding them on how they can balance the changing demands placed on them as they move away from their induction period and through their early career phase.

Within one of your early mentoring meetings, ask your mentee the following questions to deepen your understanding of their work-life balance:

- Take me through your typical working week and go through your fixed professional commitments as part of your role within the school.
- Which of these commitments do you feel has the most value?
- Which of these commitments do you feel prevent you from achieving what you want to do professionally within your role here?
- Why do you think that these commitments are asked of you?
- What do you feel that I could do to support you in your role?
- What do you feel that the school could do to support you in your role?

The responses to these questions will give you an indication of which parts of their current role they feel are supporting their own perception of their professional role within the school and those which are inhibiting this sense of their professional self.

It is important then for you to develop your understanding of what it means to be a reflexive mentor as well as continue practicing a reflexive mentoring style, as this will help you to understand the impact of your mentoring on the whole person and not just the professional behaviours that you wish to develop in them.

Being a reflexive mentor means that you have an awareness of the impact of your mentoring on yourself, the organisation in which you work and on those being mentored by yourself. As a mentor, consider the values which you model and communicate through your mentoring and how these are received by the mentee that you are working with.

Taking a step back and reflecting on the impact of your mentoring is a key developmental process for you as a mentor. Use the following prompt questions to examine your approach to your mentoring relationship:

- When you prepare for your regular mentoring meeting, what preparation do you do in advance?
- Are you always on time? How do you arrive to the meeting? Are you rushing to the meeting?
- How do you ensure that you are present and not just in the room? How do you ensure that you and your mentee are not distracted during the meeting?
- On balance, how much of a typical mentoring meeting are you talking and how much are you listening?
- If you were your mentee, what would you want to get from the meetings? Are you providing this?

As you can see from these prompt questions, the emotional space that you create and the value you place on the meetings with your mentee communicate the value that you place upon them. Mentoring is an emotional investment as well as a professional and time commitment to the development of another professional, and so you should try and develop yourself as a reflexive as well as a reflective mentor to maximize the impact that your mentoring has.

Where the mentee sees and feels the emotional, professional and time commitment that you are making as their mentor, they will know that you have their long-term professional development at the centre of the relationship that you build and sustain. This will be a key factor in helping to the retention of that member of staff within the school.

Reflective Task

- Why are mentors assigned to recently qualified teachers within a school?
- Why is it important to support your mentee to explore their career aspirations?
- How are you ensuring that your mentee is maintaining a healthy work-life balance?

Recommended Reading

Door, V. (2014), *Developing Creative and Critical Educational Practitioners*. UK: Critical Publishing.

Wason, P. C. (1960), 'On the failure to eliminate hypotheses in a conceptual task'. *The Quarterly Journal of Experimental Psychology*, 12, pp. 129–40.

Websites

A reflective guide to mentoring and being a teacher mentor (Victoria State Government 2016), https://www.education.vic.gov.au/Documents/school/teachers/profdev/Reflectiveguidetomentoringschools.pdf

References

Brockbank, A. and Mcgill, I. (2003), *The Action Learning Handbook: Powerful Techniques for Education, Professional Development and Training.* Abingdon: Routledge.
Browne, A. (2020), *Light the Way: The Case for Ethical Leadership in Schools.* UK: Bloomsbury.
Buck, A. (2020), *The BASIC Coaching Method: All You Need to Know to Coach with Confidence.* UK: Cadagon Press.
Cameron, E. and Green, M. (2019), *Making Sense of Change Management: A Complete Guide to the Models, Tools, and Techniques of Organisational Change,* 5th edn. London: Kogan Page.
Coalter, M. (2018), *Talent Architects: How to Make Your School a Great Place to Work.* UK: John Catt Publishing.
Dreyfus, S. (2004), 'The Five-Stage Model of Adult Skill Acquisition'. *Bulletin of Science Technology & Society,* 24 (10) pp. 177–79.
Durrant, J. (2019), *Teacher Agency, Professional Development and School Improvement.* Routledge.
Furlong, J. and Maynard, T. (1995), *Mentoring Student Teachers: The Growth of Professional Knowledge.* London and New York: Routledge.
Hargreaves, E. and Rolls, L. (2021), *Reimagining Professional Development in Schools: Unlocking Research.* UK: Routledge.
Lane, G. and Clutterbuck, D. (2005), *Situational Mentoring: An International Review of Competences and Capabilities in Mentoring.* UK: Sage.
Thomson, B. (2013), *Non-Directive Coaching: Attitudes, Approaches and Applications.* St. Albans: Critical Publishing.
Tomsett, J. and Uttley, J. (2020), *Putting Staff First: A Blueprint for Revitalising our Schools: A Blueprint for a Revitalised Profession.* UK: John Catt Publishing.
Weick, K. (1995), *Sensemaking in Organisations.* London: Sage.
Whitmore, J. (2019), *Coaching for Performance.* London: Brealey. Checked and edited: LO (01.09.2021)

5

Mentoring and Coaching Middle Leaders

Derek Boyle and Lizana Oberholzer

The mentoring and professional development of middle leaders is vital to the long-term capacity for a school to sustain educational standards and to implement change within the organisation. Without high-quality mentoring and coaching, schools will fail to retain the talented emerging leaders that are within their middle leaders.

Aims and Objectives

This chapter sets out to:

- Help the mentor or coach and middle leader to establish the expectations of each other within the relationship,
- Show how to support the middle leader to lead change and support their teams through the change process,
- Show how to develop the capacity and confidence of middle leaders to think operate strategically through the use of mentoring and coaching support,
- Provide advice on how to help a middle leader to explore their career aspirations while respecting their well-being and work-life balance.

Introduction

This chapter examines the pivotal relationship between members of the senior leadership team and the middle leaders within the school. This relationship is paramount if existing outcomes are going to be sustained or improvements made, as the middle leader within each school is the engine of change (Bentley-Davies, 2017; NCTL, 2003; Robbins, 2021). Middle leaders are the operational leadership wing of the school that can directly affect change in the behaviours of the teachers within the school, and this must be recognized. Middle leaders within school settings are the enablers of the strategic vision expressed and conveyed by the senior leadership team (NCTL, 2003; Robbins, 2021). In this way they are pivotal to the success of the organisation, and their development is key to any school enacting change or sustaining excellence. Developing this relationship through mentoring and coaching will implement the strategic vision originating from the head teacher and governing board or trustee board to be enacted within each team.

The line management of middle leaders is built upon an understanding of the pressures that you will be placing upon them consciously and unconsciously as well as the stresses they are under as a result of the personalities within their teams and their own internally originated pressures (Cameron and Green, 2019). Middle leaders are very much 'stuck in the middle' of the competing pressures and demands placed upon them. Managing their own perceptions of success and failure is key to developing them as leaders and managers.

When you take on the line management of a single middle leader (or a whole team of them), you will need to take on both a mentoring and a coaching role in order to get the best out of them and their associated teams. It is important to be aware of how to move on the continuum of coaching and mentoring, as described in Chapters 1 and 4, to ensure that you can support the leaders in your care in a mindful and supportive way. All middle leaders will not be at the same stage of their leadership journey, and it might be that they need different support. It is therefore important to get to know your team well, put yourself in their shoes (Browne, 2020) and reflect on how you can support them through the use of mentoring and coaching as cognitive leadership approaches suggest (Cameron and Green, 2020). As well as knowing your team well, you also need to reflect on the different middle leadership types. Within this chapter we will examine how to mentor and coach four different 'types' of middle leaders.

The Middle Leadership Types

Type A: is the newly promoted middle leader who has inherited an existing team but has little leadership experience. In the light of the Dreyfus model (2004) Type A – middle leaders are novices on their leadership journey and often benefit most from being mentors at the outset of their journey.

Type B: is the recently promoted middle leader who has a good understanding of their team. These colleagues are often at the advance beginner phrase and are starting to progress into the proficient stage, and the mentor or coach needs to reflect on how they need to move on the continuum of mentoring and coaching to support this colleague best as they move towards greater independents and confidence.

Type C: is the experienced middle leader who has a relatively stable team but wants to develop them further. These colleagues are often highly confident, and a coaching approach is key to help facilitate their learning.

Type D: is the experienced middle leader who does not yet have their team working either coherently or competently. Depending on the challenges and stages, the support needs to be evaluated in line with the needs of this leader, and Blanchard et al.'s (2018) situational leadership model outlines how support needs to be carefully considered for the middle leader to ensure that they are best supported as seen in the adaptation in Figure 5.1.

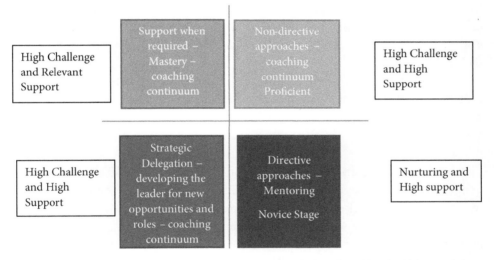

Figure 5.1 An adaptation of Blanchard et al.'s (2018) situational leadership model.

The support needs to be carefully considered in relation to when to be director or mentor, when to coach and when to offer support, as well as when to delegate strategically

Although the Situational Leadership model suggested by Blanchard (2018) gives a recommendation as to how we can progress leaders through a *directing-coaching-supporting-delegating* pathway, the authors propose a model that utilizes the idea of mentoring and coaching behaviours being on a continuum that aligns more closely with the Dreyfus model (2004) of adult skill acquisition.

Figure 5.2 A model utilising the idea of mentoring and coaching behaviours being on continuum (Blanchard et al., 2018).

When working with middle leaders, your role in supporting their development will require the adaptation of your own approach through a number of distinct phases as they gain confidence and then competence in their role.

The contextual mentoring phase will be used when the middle leader is in the 'novice' phase within the Dreyfus model (2004) and this is centred on the development of confidence and helping them to explore the bounds and possibilities of the role. This stage is linked to helping the mentee to discover the bounds of their self-agency within this role.

As the mentee develops critical self-reflection and becomes more reflexive in their professional behaviours, the relationship that you have with them moves to a coaching model. The use of enabling questions and silence to help the mentee transition to a coachee within the relationship is a key point for the evolving professional relationship.

As an extension of the coaching relationship, we want the middle leader to start questioning their own practice through utilising the learning questions approach proposed by Clutterbuck and Lane (2005) explored in Chapter 2. Working with them to explore not only the *what* and *how* of the strategies that they are developing to manage their role, but *why* they are proposing courses of action leads to a consolidation of the conviction as to the right course of action they are wishing to take. This part of the model is linked to the proficient stage of the Dreyfus model. The importance of neutral and non-judgemental questions within this stage to explore the *why* is a key approach that must be utilized within this stage.

The final stage of this model is akin to the mastery level of the Dreyfus model, and this is where you encourage the middle leader to practice the approaches that you have modelled for them in the earlier stages with members of their own team or a novice middle leader from outside of their own team.

Returning to our four types of middle leaders, each of these types of middle leaders require different skills, approaches and planning to develop them further.

Reflective Task

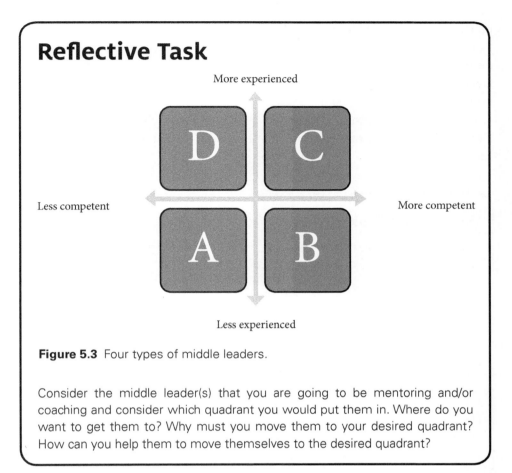

Figure 5.3 Four types of middle leaders.

Consider the middle leader(s) that you are going to be mentoring and/or coaching and consider which quadrant you would put them in. Where do you want to get them to? Why must you move them to your desired quadrant? How can you help them to move themselves to the desired quadrant?

Making Expectations Clear

In the initial meeting with your middle leader, what do you want to get out of the meeting as a mentor or coach now and then in subsequent meetings?

If you are new to the school as a leader, and the middle leader is already established or internally promoted to their position, they will have a deeper cultural understanding of the organisation than yourself. This may give rise to responses such as 'well we have always done this in that way ….' or 'with my last line manager we agreed ….' For those coming from another school, they may use phrases such as 'At my last school …' and this will immediately lead to concerns over competing cultures within the middle leader that will need to be addressed. However, it is also important to acknowledge that there is prior expertise and knowledge, which can be tapped into, and celebrated. Always make sure that you convey that you value what the middle leader brings to the table, and that you are prepared to work with them, to identify the next steps, to meet the needs of the learners, the organisation as well as the areas of focus (Adair, 2009).

Going into this meeting without pre-planning will result in you being on the back foot and establishing 'cultural norms' in this relationship that will be hard to unpick later.

> **Reflective Task**
>
> Think about your new middle leader and consider planning your next meeting with them using the following prompts:
>
> 1. What is the historical context of the performance of their department or team? Has that been down to them or a previous middle leader?
> 2. Who was their previous line manager? What sort of relationship did they have?
> 3. What outcomes do you want to get from this first meeting?
> 4. How frequently are you going to meet? Where will the meeting take place?
> 5. Where must you get the team to? What expectations are placed on you for their collective performance by your line manager? How long have you got to demonstrate this change?
> 6. Are your expectations and targets that are subsequently agreed going to be linked to performance management?

When to Coach and When to Mentor

If we consider mentoring and coaching as a continuum, different aspects of the work that you will be doing with your middle leader will fall somewhere along this line, as reflected on in Chapters 1 and 4 (Buck, 2020).

For a new member of staff to the school who is also new into this role (Type A from above) they may need a lot of intensive mentoring and support both from yourself and from their team. What functional aspects of their role do they need to know now and what can be left for a few weeks?

Type B might be someone who has been promoted internally and they will need support in establishing a change in perception from their colleagues. Strong personal friendships and established relationships will need to evolve when this person steps up to their new role. Managing this changing relationship with colleagues will need a mixture of mentoring and coaching approaches. The leader will need to reflect on how to shape their new identity and establish themselves in their new role. By providing a safe learning space, the middle leader can work out through the mentor or coach on how to make sense of these challenges (Weick, 1995).

Type C is an experienced middle leader, who has a good understanding of their team, and it is your responsibility to help them to develop themselves further. This will require a coaching approach and working alongside them to explore how they feel that they want to develop themselves and their teams. However, as explored in the above, looking at Blanchard et al.'s (2018) model, you might also strategically start delegating challenges to this middle leader to start preparing them for future roles as senior leaders. Exploring ways in which you can both identify the next steps for the middle leader and facilitate opportunities for each member of the team will enable them all to feel valued, and their loyalty to their organisation, and to yourself, will be enhanced.

Type D is an experienced middle leader who does not have their team where they want them to be yet. This could be for a number of reasons, such as staff turnover for promotion, retention issues, staff recruited on short-term contracts because of in-year resignations, retirements, caring leave or staff bordering on competency proceedings. This type of middle leader will need careful and considerate handling as they will tend to feel deflated and not in control of their teams. Using a mentoring approach may make them feel patronized, unless you have identified very specific support mechanisms that they will need help with developing. A coaching approach where you both carefully identify the issues that need addressing within the team and the practical steps that you as the line manager can take to support the middle leader might be the way forward, unless there are potential issues with his/her own practices which require a different mode of support, such as mentoring. Soothing words without any practical steps to achieve the change that you have both identified will impact negatively on the well-being of your middle leader. In addition, having clear targets, goals and direction, with clear support and autonomy, will be highly motivating (Pink, 2018). Creating conditions of high challenge and low threat will enable leaders to thrive (Myatt, 2016).

Mentoring Middle Leaders to Lead Change

To enable your middle leader to lead on change, they will need to have an internal self-belief that they can accomplish this task and that it is supported by the leaders above them. Building their self-confidence in their own decision making and giving leaders autonomy and agency are key and will encourage them to carry their team with them (Pink, 2018).

Within your relationship with them, you should encourage them to challenge the parameters of decisions made by the senior leadership team in an appropriate form, which will enable them to develop a feeling of common endeavour that the change is valued and looked for by the leadership of the school. Working with others as collaborative professionals will enable leaders to build strong foundations to lead (Hargreaves and O'Connor, 2018). This will build a relationship based on trust between the middle and senior leadership of the school showing that the effort that will be made to manage and lead change will be valued.

When establishing the parameters for the desired change, consider the time needed to complete the change. This will be based on the perceived time that was expected and the actual time that it takes. Be aware of the amount of time that the internalisation of the process to effect change takes and that the middle leader will need opportunities to discuss and rationalize the steps to success that they will need to take (Weick, 1995).

Leading change is in addition to the amount of time and resilience needed to manage the operational demands of leading the middle leader's team. Monitoring the personal workload of the middle leader should be a high priority for any line manager, and this is part of the mentoring approach that you will need to take in supporting them (Coalter, 2018).

The mental resilience of the middle leader is going to be key to their success in leading change. Helping them to manage the known demands and having the reserves to deal with external, unforeseen demands, such as staff absence, sickness, underperformance, parental complaints and caring responsibilities, is part of your role.

Look for changes in their well-being over time, and consider the timelines and deadlines that you give them for turning around the operational demands of their roles. If the school is expecting monitoring of the implementation of policies and procedures by their team, do they have the capacity and resilience to provide an update at two days' notice on the strategic development they are leading on?

Mentoring Middle Leaders to Support Teams

If your middle leader is working with an existing team of teachers and support staff, both of you will need to have a detailed and accurate picture of their relative strengths, experience, expertise and areas for development. A complicating factor will be if the middle leader has been promoted internally or has a long association with them personally and professionally. This needs to be undertaken in a detached and almost clinical approach, as the emotional investment that all parties within the team will have with each other will colour the analysis.

Taking each member in turn, jointly write a short professional biography of each team member and conclude this with two aspirations for each member. What do they want to achieve professionally and what does the middle leader want them to achieve over the coming twelve months?

This process will give the middle leader a good starting point to write a development plan for their team and look for new opportunities for them for the coming twelve months. Come back to this development plan at each of your meetings, and review how they are progressing against the plan that the middle leader has developed.

If the middle leader is taking on a new team, or they have little prior knowledge of them professionally, groundwork will need to be undertaken by the new middle leader for them to gain insights into the team. It might also be worth reflecting with the middle leader on how they utilize mentoring and coaching strategies to support their own team.

Time will need to be found for the middle leader to meet with each of their team members and gather information on their teaching experience to date, course or subject specific knowledge and what their perceive as their areas for development. Encouraging the middle leader to have detailed discussions in protected time will enable the team to bond as a group.

Mentoring Middle Leaders to Address Difficult Situations

Middle leaders must deal with concerns that are not only expressed in a variety of ways by their teams but also from pupils, their parents or carers and support staff. If these concerns become confrontational, the middle leader will need an opportunity to discuss strategies and seek advice, before, during and afterwards.

If middle leaders are spending time dealing with confrontation or communication originating from classroom issues, these need monitoring and discussing before they become escalated by parents or carers (Robbins, 2021). Persistent parents or carers can have a debilitating effect on middle leaders and their teams, preventing them from dealing with the original issues.

During your meetings, spend time gaining an insight on the number of issues that the middle leader is dealing with that involve home contact. It is important to gain a clearer sense of the range of issues the middle leader is dealing with and workload tensions for the middle leader. If these are with a small number of parents or carers, ask if it might be helpful to co-chair a meeting with the concerned parent or carer to bring the issue to a conclusion with an agreed set of actions, as a modelling and learning opportunity.

You should have an agreed communications policy within your school, but the implementation of it will need monitoring and discussing (Tomsett and Uttley, 2020).

You should decide on how much contextual information you should share with parents or carers? Do you always stick to the 'school line' and defend the handling of situations in all situations? Discuss with your middle leader about when they should deal with issues themselves, when to pass it up to you and when to pass the issue back to the class teacher to deal with. Having agreed procedures to deal with recurrent complaints and/or communication from parents will help your middle leader to navigate and improve their decision-making processes.

It is always prudent to remember to explain when good is good enough to the middle leader and that you cannot please all of the people all of the time. It is important as a colleague supporting your middle leader to be aware of the impact of negative bias (Grenville-Cleave, 2016) and to help develop the middle leader's self-awareness of how negative bias can have an impact and how to think of strategies to also celebrate successes and positives to ensure that the middle leader remains motivated, positive and engaged.

The role of the senior leader, mentor or coach is to care for and manage the pressures on the middle leader.

Mentoring Middle Leaders to Lead Strategically

If you are considering asking your middle leader to work strategically, what does this mean? Within most schools this will mean becoming involved with a cross-school project or initiative, but is this truly working strategically?

Strategic leadership refers to a leader's potential to express a strategic vision for the organisation, or a part of the organisation, and to motivate and persuade others to acquire that vision. Buck (2016) highlights that once the vision is shared, the leader needs to make sure that all stakeholders participate in the vision. Crawford et al. (2000) highlight that a vision must be communicated in a way which secures commitment among members of the organisation. Crawford et al. (2000) outline that the vision or intentions need to be compelling and pull people toward them.

Before you embark on finding ways for the middle leader to think and act more strategically, have you considered if the middle leader has the desire or drive to work strategically across the school? Is it necessary for their role? If it is not, how do you get 'buy-in' from them? However, if we look critically at the definitions, it can also be that they need to work strategically with their teams, and it is therefore important to help develop the leader's ability to develop their strategic thinking around supporting their own area and team. Within the constrained structures found within schools, how can you facilitate the space for them to establish and maintain systems, allocate resources and communicate vision while maintaining a focus on the central vision for the school?

> **Reflective Task**
>
> Consider one of the whole school priorities that you wish your middle leader to work strategically on and answer the following questions:
>
> - What will success look like to you?
> - What will success look like to the middle leader?
> - How will success benefit and grow the middle leader?
> - How will it help them to grow and develop their team?
> - How can this development be rolled out across the wider school community?
> - What is the purpose of the task? Does it have a true strategic value?
> - Who will take credit for this development?

If the answer to this last question is positive, and it is you, as the leader, responsible for the initiative, you need to reflect on why you are asking your middle leaders to undertake this additional work in the first place.

The mentoring process will involve building trust between yourself and your middle leader so that the additional work and tension with their team will be worthwhile. The benefits to them, their team and the wider school community need to be communicated clearly and understood by both of you. Actively listen to their concerns about resources and time as these are usually the tip of the iceberg, and there are many deeper concerns that they are not yet ready to share. Active listening is key to reflect that you are truly hearing your middle leader, value their perspective and empathize with their challenges, and it ensures that you are willing to work with them to find solutions as collaborative professionals (Hargreaves and O'Connor, 2018). Active listening can be as simple as playing back what you have heard, summarising and paraphrasing key points by using phrases such as 'what I am hearing is …', 'can I just play this back to you …' or 'I can see that this is really challenging for you; what will be the most helpful thing to consider first?'

Look back at your responses to the questions above and reflect on the answers that you gave. Now put yourself in the position of your middle leader and ask yourself, Have I got the capacity to think differently and effect change? Consider the normal workload on the middle leader and what could you do to give them the space to think, grow and develop their approaches to the initiative that you want them to work on.

Establish a way in which the middle leaders can get together either in pairs or small groups where they can provide each other with a non-threatening sounding board. Allow them time to grow and construct approaches to balance the desire from you to get them to think strategically, balance the needs of their teams and become comfortable with changes that will have to be enacted.

You will also need to give the middle leader a feeling of ownership of this new strategy, while realising that it has to be commissioned and executed within a constrained structure.

In the National College of School Leadership (NCLT) 2003 report 'The Role and Purpose of middle leaders in Schools', it identified two tensions which impact on the work of middle leaders:

1 between senior staff expectations that the middle leader would play a whole-school role and a common belief among middle leaders that their loyalty was to their department or subject responsibilities,
2 between a developing line management culture within a hierarchical school structure and a belief in collegiality.

These tensions are as true today as when this chapter was written. Expecting middle leaders to work strategically across the whole school is in direct tension with the wish of the middle leader to develop and grow their own team. However, it is also true that some middle leaders will become future senior leaders, and the mentor or coach need to have the needs of each individual middle leader in mind to help develop and unlock their potential to enable them to flourish.

If you are encouraging or expecting your middle leader to take on a whole school project or responsibility so that they can 'work strategically', how will it benefit their team or them?

Developing a collegiate sense among the middle leader team is important so that they can develop a support network where they can share thoughts, fears, anxieties, ideas and aspirations in a non-threatening environment. Having a safe collaborative professional space in place will ensure that leaders can learn from each other and strengthen their practice as part of a learning community (Hargreaves and O'Connor, 2018).

When you are the line manager and appraiser for performance management as well as the mentor or coach, it can be difficult for the middle leader to share anxieties about how your wish for them to 'work strategically' will impact on their ability or capacity to manage and lead their team.

Mentoring Middle Leaders to Use SMART Data to Shape Their Planning

Ask yourself, why does the school collect data on pupils? Who is it for? What is done with the data? What value is placed on the data? Who is held accountable because of this data? Why are they held accountable? Who checks that the data is accurate and reliable?

Once you have reflected on and considered your own answers to these questions, consider the workload that is generated in collecting this data for the middle leaders and their teams.

Discuss with your middle leader what data is to be collected and how it is going to improve teaching and learning through shaping the planning for each class and pupil within the classes. If the data that is collected cannot be used to improve the planning at a pupil, class or year group level, then you need to be asking why it is being collected. If there is little value in the data that is being collected, then a discussion needs to be had at the senior leadership level within the school.

Mentoring and Coaching Middle Leaders to Lead on Appraisals

Every school will have an appraisal or performance management process, usually annually, but often there will interim opportunities to reflect on progress, and this is linked to performance management as a process of holding staff and stakeholders to account for specific agreed objectives.

Where whole school objectives are embedded into performance management or appraisal targets as a strategic approach to ensure that core issues are addressed, this will be cascaded down through the leadership structure. Outcome driven objectives will be set from the top and then apportioned to the relevant middle leader, who will be responsible for their implementation at a team level.

A key consideration is how are you, as the senior leader, going to ensure consistency in the approach that is used across the school by all the middle leaders?

For the middle leader to be able to lead on the appraisal process at a team level, they will need mentoring through the process if it is their first time undertaking this with their own team. Even experienced middle leaders will need coaching as to how this can be achieved because the personalities and competencies of those within the team evolve over time.

A mentoring approach can be used if the middle leader is lacking experience, and this is going to be based on the lessons that they learn from your own appraisal process interview with them. When reviewing the past performance of the middle leader, you will be establishing the context of how the appraisal and target setting process is going to be framed. This will be modelling to the middle leader the expectations that you have for how they will be working with members of their own team.

When you are preparing for the appraisal, ask the middle leader to review their own performance before the meeting and think about targets that will be supportive of the whole school objectives and those that will help them develop professionally.

This approach can then be modelled by the middle leader when they prepare for the interviews with members of their own team.

If the middle leader is more confident in leading the appraisal process with their team members, a coaching approach can be utilized based upon a discussion of the relevant strengths and areas for development across the team. This discussion can be then used to plan for which members of the team can be thought of the initiators of any changes that the middle leader wants to accomplish and those members of the team that will need additional mentoring or coaching.

Mentoring and Coaching Middle Leaders on Developing Their Career Plan

Within your regular line management meetings, you will soon get a sense of the goals and aspirations of your Middle leader, but remember to ask them regularly about their career plans and what you can do to help them achieve it. A sensible time to instigate these conversations would be before the appraisal process and at mid-year review points. The following prompt questions can be used to frame this discussion.

> ### Reflective Task
> - What do you most enjoy about your current role?
> - What do you feel holds you back from achieving everything you want to in your current role?
> - If you could make one change to your current role, what would it be?
> - What do you want to achieve in your role?
> - What could the school do to help you feel more fulfilled?
> - Where do you see yourself and your team this time next year?
> - Thinking about the strategic direction of the school, name one thing that should stay the same and one thing that could change?
> - What are your career aspirations, and how could the school help you achieve them?

Within the discussion you will have to balance what is best for the career development of the middle leader and what is best for the school. Sometimes you will have the dilemma of a very competent middle leader, who can be relied on to deliver excellent outcomes for their pupils, but who also wants to move up or sideways into another role, which puts at risk those excellent outcomes. Managing a process whereby other members of the team can be developed to step into the place of the middle leader if they advance their career will be critical in coaching them along their desired career path.

Where and when you discover the career aspirations of your middle leader(s), share them with your headteacher so that they become part of a wider discussion as to other opportunities that can be engineered to retain excellent talent within your school.

Taking an interest and developing talent within your middle leader team will help to build mutual respect, as they will feel valued and will retain the trust and good will to follow you.

The following task will help you to develop a good understanding of the career aspirations of your middle leader.

Task

Ask your middle leader to think about and respond to the following questions:

Strengths

- What do you consider to be your strengths in your current role?
- What are the strengths of your team?

Weaknesses

- Which aspects of your role do you feel least sure about?
- What don't you have time to do?

Opportunities

- What are your professional areas of interest?
- What would you like to develop but do not have the time to?
- What would you like to develop, but you are not sure about how to do it?
- What would you like to be doing differently next year?
- Where do you see the next step in your professional career?

Threats

- What do you consider to be holding you back from achieving what you want to with your team?
- If we could make one change across the school, what would it be and why?

The answers to these questions can form the basis of future discussions about how your middle leader can start framing their career aspirations and what steps you can take to help them realize these aspirations.

Mentoring and Coaching Middle Leaders on Exploring Senior Leadership Roles

Some schools look to develop their middle leader team through helping them to explore senior leadership roles by incorporating them into an associate senior leadership group. This can be a valuable experience, either through a leadership restructuring exercise, temporary secondment or through building additional capacity within the senior leadership team. However, for members of the middle leadership, the benefits must be considered against the additional time pressures that will be placed on them.

Consider why you want the middle leader to experience working as part of the extended senior leadership team. What is the benefit to them, the existing senior leadership team and the wider school?

You must consider the existing workload and associated non-teaching expectations (detentions, parental contact, data monitoring and interpretation, monitoring and development of Schemes of Learning, learning walks, lesson observations, checking of book marking) and then what extra expectations are placed on the middle leader with this new enhanced role. Any additional meetings and duties expected of the member of the associate senior leadership teams reduce the time they have in-school to manage and lead their existing team. When considering helping your middle leader to explore senior leadership roles, consider that for every additional workload inducing responsibility, what can you reduce, remove or delegate to someone else?

Wider experience across the school is developmental for the middle leader, but will it impact on their work-life balance?

Task

You have been asked by your line manager to invite the middle leader to become part of the extended senior leadership team within the school. Think about each of the following questions and write down your thoughts for this scenario.

1 What questions do you need to ask your line manager?
2 What questions are you likely to get from your middle leader?
3 What additional workload will this entail?
4 What can you do to reduce the wider workload of your middle leader for the additional commitments they will be expected to make each week?
5 Will the extra commitments impact on any caring responsibilities of your middle leader?

> You can think of this as a cost-benefit analysis type approach to this scenario with the welfare and wider professional development of the middle leader as the focus.
>
> On reflection, what are the overall costs and benefits to the middle leader of them becoming part of an extended senior leadership team group?

Facilitating Thinking

As a line manager to a middle leader, what do you do to give them time to stop and think about their role? Developing reflective practice in your middle leader is going to depend on the opportunities for them to pause and catch their breath that you facilitate. Are there peer support mechanisms that can be set up for them to work with other middle leaders to pause and reflect on their pressures and to evolve mechanisms to come up with innovative solutions to common problems? Who sets the agenda for middle leader group meetings? Do these have to be driven from the senior leadership team, or could they be decided on in consultation with the wider leadership in the school?

Case Study

The following case study has been provided by Mary Myatt and illustrates the need for those who are mentoring and supporting middle leaders to address the culture within the organisation and to model the ideal response to change and perceived threats.

An AD HOC programme to support middle leaders provided feedback to colleagues after observing lessons and looking at books. This was identified as a need because a culture of fear had developed relating to this aspect of school improvement.

It was agreed that the middle leaders should work to the principles of 'high challenge' accompanied by 'low threat'. This draws on the insight that we like doing things that stretch us but are fearful of being made to look stupid. The sessions included practising phrases that would take the heat out of the situation, and which would also reveal more information.

The coaching sessions consisted of outlining the principles of 'high challenge, low threat'. This draws on the argument that we are a challenge-seeking species; we like doing things that are difficult. However, we do not want to be made to feel stupid when things go wrong. We do our best work when we are psychologically free from the fear of making mistakes. One helpful strategy is to focus on the work rather than the person. To do this, we practized using 'distancing' phrases so that the conversations focused on the substance of the work in a dispassionate manner. For example, instead of 'I liked this part of the lesson' to 'When you provided this activity, pupils were responding with thoughtful observations and questions'. And instead of 'That lesson required improvement' phrase it as 'When the class were not paying attention, do you think there are some phrases that could bring them back to focus? Shall we work together to practice some of those?'

The impact of this work meant that both the middle leaders and the colleagues they were working with said that conversations about the quality of learning were more open and honest.

The unintended consequence of this light touch reframing of the processes relating to quality assurance was that the middle leaders modelled the 'distancing' phrasing with their colleagues. They agreed that they felt more confident about holding themselves and others to account in a way that was both robust and kind. This way of working means that colleagues are more open about aspects of their practice of which they are proud, without being boastful, and conversely are more prepared to be open about what is not working so well. This is because the sting and potential psychological threat has been taken out of the process. It shifted the professional atmosphere from potential blame and judgement to one of open discussion about what makes the greatest difference to pupils' learning.

A further element of impact of this work was that colleagues had insights into the wider implications of framing feedback in this more humane way in the classroom: they realized that they could use this when providing feedback to pupils on their work – rather than praising or admonishing the pupil as an individual, they focused on the strengths and areas for development. They reported that pupils were more engaged in developing their work when they created the conditions of 'high challenge and low threat'.

Considering the Well-Being of the Middle Leader (ML)

When you have taken on the mentoring and coaching of a middle leader, you need to put their well-being at the centre of what you do. The burnout and loss of experienced middle leaders is paralysing for their teams, and the rebuilding of the team and their confidence in the leadership of the school to look after them will be severely impacted. If the school is then looking to replace a middle leader by internally promoting them, what life lessons have they been taught if the previous post holder has not been looked after? If talent is sought externally, what are you going to tell interview candidates about why the previous post-holder has left?

Table 5.1 Six elements of psychological well-being (Westerhof and Keyes 2009)

Element	Considerations for mentoring
1. Self-acceptance: a positive and acceptant attitude towards aspects of self, in past and present.	How can you show the confidence that the school had in the ML when they were appointed? How can you help the ML to reflect on the skills and experiences that they bring with them and how they can be applied to this new role?
2. Purpose in life: goals and beliefs that affirm a sense of direction and meaning in life.	What does the new ML want to achieve with their team? Which of these are verbalized from the internal sense of direction that the ML has, and which are imposed by the hierarchical structure within the school?
3. Autonomy: self-direction as guided by one's own socially accepted internal standards.	To what extent can the ML have control and autonomy over the functional and strategic leadership of their team?
4. Positive relations with others: having satisfying personal relationships in which empathy and intimacy are expressed.	Within the ML team, who can provide peer coaching and mentoring to manage systems and expectations in a non-threatening way? What can you do as the 'formal coach' to help the new ML understand the personalities and departmental politics?
5. Environmental mastery: the capability to manage the complex environment according to one's own needs.	The environment in which the ML is working is subject to formal and informal rules, policies and procedures. Established practice within a department can be the hardest aspect of a culture that has been established over time to comprehend and navigate. What can you do to help them shape and adapt these environmental factors to improve their well-being?
6. Personal growth: the insight into one's own potential for self-development.	What are their short-term personal goals? How can you get them to articulate these?

Well-being can be considered in three main domains: psychological, social and emotional.

Psychological well-being can be broken down into the following six elements (Westerhof and Keyes, 2009).

Another aspect highlighted by the work of Westerhof and Keyes (2009) was the consideration of the social well-being of people within society, and this can be adapted to consider the social well-being of your middle leader. This work was originated by Ryff (1989), and we can consider the how societal norms are correlated

> **Task**
>
> Consider one of your middle leaders and reflect on what you actively do to consider their psychological well-being based on your expectations of them. What could you actively do to improve their well-being?

with the society within the school that they work in, and we can apply the elements of Westerhof and Keyes work.

Ensuring that the new ML can integrate to the social norms within the leadership and management culture within the school is important for their sense of identity and place.

Social well-being can be broken down into five linked elements:

1. Social coherence: being able to make meaning of what is happening in society.
2. Social acceptance: a positive attitude toward others while acknowledging their difficulties.
3. Social actualisation: the belief that the community has potential and can evolve positively.
4. Social contribution: the feeling that one's activities contribute to and are valued by society.
5. Social integration: a sense of belonging to a community.

Linking these to the school environment, we can then consider our response as mentors and coaches to these:

Table 5.2 Mentors and coaches' responses to elements of social well-being

Aspect	Prompts
1. Social coherence: being able to make meaning of what is happening in the school society.	What is their place in that society? Who can they turn to when facing difficulties?
2. Social acceptance: a positive attitude toward others while acknowledging their difficulties.	How can we provide an opportunity for them to share openly the successes and challenges that people working within the school face?
3. Social actualisation: the belief that the community has potential and can evolve positively.	How is the vision for the school developed, shared and articulated? Who has control of the drivers of change within the school society?
4. Social contribution: the feeling that one's activities contribute to and are valued by society.	How can their voice be heard and valued in middle leader's meetings and in their meetings with you?
5. Social integration: a sense of belonging to a community.	Is there an opportunity for the middle leader to become part of or form a community and forum for discussion among peers?

> **Reflective Task**
>
> 1 Using the prompt questions from Table 5.2, what are you actively doing to nurture the social well-being of your middle leader?
> 2 What will be the impact on the middle leader if you do not take their social well-being into account?

Recommended Reading

Campbell, J. and van Nieuwerburgh, C. (2018), *The Leader's Guide to Coaching in Schools: Creating Conditions for Effective Learning*. UK: Corwin.

Education Support Partnership (2021), 'Teacher wellbeing index 2021' [WWW Document]. Available at: https://www.educationsupport.org.uk/media/5pgbh1bn/twix_2021_3_mental_health_of_education_staff.pdf

'Teaching council of New Zealand'. Available at: https://teachingcouncil.nz/content/very-real-value-of-teacher-wellbeing

'Ofsted report summary on teacher well-being'. Available at: https://www.gov.uk/government/publications/teacher-well-being-at-work-in-schools-and-further-education-providers/summary-and-recommendations-teacher-well-being-research-report

The full report is available at: https://assets.publishing.service.gov.uk/government/uploads/system/uploads/attachment_data/file/819314/Teacher_well-being_report_110719F.pdf

'Guardian interview with a headteacher on the importance of well-being'. Available at: https://www.theguardian.com/teacher-network/teacher-blog/2013/jul/01/school-staff-wellbeing-headteacher-leaders

Ryff, C. D. (1989), 'Happiness is everything, or is it? Explorations on the meaning of psychological well-being'. *Journal of Personality and Social Psychology*, 57, pp. 1069–81.

References

Adair, J. (2009), *The Inspirational Leader: How to Motivate, Encourage and Achieve Success* (The John Adair Leadership Library). UK: Kogan Page.

Bentley-Davies, C. (2017), *How to Be an Amazing Middle Leader*. UK: Crown House.

Blanchard K. Fowler S. and Hawkins, L. (2018), *Self-Leadership and the One Minute Manager, Gain the Mindset and Skillset for Getting What You Need to Succeed*. London: Harper Thorsons.

Browne, A. (2020), *Light the Way: The Case for Ethical Leadership in Schools*. UK: Bloomsbury.

Buck, A. (2016), *Leadership Matters*. UK: John Catt Publication.

Buck, A. (2020), *The BASIC Coaching Method: All You Need to Know to Coach with Confidence*. UK: Cadogan Press.

Cameron, E. and Green, M. (2019), *Making Sense of Change Management: A Complete Guide to the Models, Tools, and Techniques of Organisational Change*, 5th edn. London: Kogan Page.

Campbell, J. and van Nieuwerburgh, C. (2018), *The Leader's Guide to Coaching in Schools: Creating Conditions for Effective Learning*. UK: Corwin.

Cherkowski, S. (2018), 'Positive teacher leadership: Building mindsets and capacities to grow wellbeing'. *International Journal of Teacher Leadership* 9(1), Spring 2018. Available at: https://files.eric.ed.gov/fulltext/EJ1182707.pdf (Accessed: 01.09.2021).

Coalter, M. (2018), *Talent Architects: How to Make Your School a Great Place to Work*. UK: John Catt Publishing.

Crawford, M., Kydd, L. and Riches, C. (2000), *Leadership and Teams in Educational Management*. UK: OU.

Dreyfus, S. (204), 'The five-stage model of adult skill acquisition, bulletin of science'. *Technology & Society*, 24(3), June 2004, pp. 177–81. Available at: Dreyfus-skill-level.pdf (bu.edu) (Accessed: 01.06.2021).

Grenville-Cleave, B. (2016), *Positive Psychology: A Toolkit for Happiness, Purpose and Well-Being*. UK: Icon Books Ltd.

Hargreaves, A. and O'Connor, M. T. (2018), *Collaborative Professionalism: When Teaching Together Means Learning for All*. UK: Corwin.

Lane, G. and Clutterbuck, D. (2005), *Situational Mentoring: An International Review of Competences and Capabilities in Mentoring*. UK: Sage.

Myatt, M. (2016), *High Challenge Low Risk*. UK: John Catt Publishing.

NCSL (2003), The Role and Purpose of Middle Leaders in Schools, Stationer Office: DfE. Available at: The role and purpose of middle leaders in schools (ioe.ac.uk) (Accessed: 01.09.2021).

Pink, D. (2018), *Drive: The Surprising Truth about What Motivates Us*. UK: Canongate Books.

Robbins, A. (2021), *Middle Leadership Mastery: A Toolkit for Subject and Pastoral Leaders*. UK: Crown House.

Tomsett, J. and Uttley, J. (2020), *Putting Staff First: A Blueprint for Revitalising Our Schools: A Blueprint for a Revitalised Profession*. UK: John Catt Publishing.

Weick, K. (1995), *Sensemaking in Organisations*. London: Sage.

Westerhof, G. J. and Keyes, C. L. M. (2009), 'Mental Illness and Mental Health: The Two Continua Model across the Lifespan', Springerlink.com Available at: 10.1007/s10804-009-9082-y.pdf (springer.com) (Accessed: 01.09.2021).

6

Mentoring and Coaching Senior Leaders

Derek Boyle and Lizana Oberholzer

Aims and Objectives

In this chapter we will be examining ways in which you can mentor and coach a new member of the Senior Leadership Team (SLT) within your school. At this level, the focus of mentoring and coaching needs to be balanced across several different areas:

- The operational nuances of the school in which they will be working and how to leverage engagement and delivery from the teams that they are supporting,
- The stepping up to a visible leadership role where they will be part of the corporate face of the school,
- Supporting senior leaders to develop and articulate strategy so that it can be realized,
- Leading several different teams.

Introduction

When leaders are promoted to join the senior leadership team within a school, they are being adopted into the inner circle that drives and leads change within the organization. The mentoring and coaching of these new members of the 'engine room' within the school is vital if the culture and ethos of the community that they will now be working within is to flourish. As the new members of the senior leadership team become integrated into the school the focus for those providing the mentoring is to move to a coaching model which will help to develop their capacity to lead change within the organization.

If the school is part of a Multi-Academy Trust (MAT), then opportunities will open up for the newly inducted members of SLT to take on wider leadership and collaborative roles across the organisation too.

Making Expectations Clear

When inducting a new member of SLT into an existing team, their ability to assimilate the culture and ethos of the school quickly is important, but consider what else was seen at the interview stage that made them a good addition to the team. What additional skills do they bring to the table, and how can their unique selling points also extend and help to develop the team? Help them to unlock these qualities.

While making the expectations of the school clear is important that the wider skills, experiences and drive that attracted them to the role need to be nurtured too. In addition, it is important to discuss the importance of leadership values, and the expectations set out in the Nolan Principles or public life which are:

- Selflessness
- Integrity
- Objectivity
- Accountability
- Openness
- Honesty
- Leadership

It is important for the new senior leader to understand that they do not only need to uphold their own values but that of their school as well, in line with the demands of the role. It is important that the SLT member feel that they can be authentic in their leadership and true to themselves, as well as support their school with conviction.

As mentioned in previous chapters, at this stage, the senior leader needs to work with their mentor or coach to establish which stage of the journey they are at. If they are in a complete novice stage, it might often be best to be supported in a mentoring capacity first to ease into the role as highlighted by Dreyfus (2004) and Blanchard et al. (2018). It is often helpful to explain to the senior leader how working on the continuum of mentoring and coaching will help them to develop on their journey and become more confident and grow into their role.

When to Coach and When to Mentor

The transition from a mentoring approach to a coaching approach is going to be unique for every member of the SLT that joins the team, but this will be an investment that needs careful thought and management. If a senior leader is completely new to their role, it might mean that the journey to progress to coaching will take slightly longer, as they need to move through the novice and advance beginner stages first, and a more directive approach will be more helpful; however, as they become more independent, they will start moving into the independent or 'winding down' zone, as outlined by Clutterbuck and Lane (2005), where re-contracting needs to take place and a coaching approach is introduced. However, even during the coaching relationships, it might be that there are moments where the coach will need to move on the continuum of mentoring and coaching to offer mentor support with the senior leader's permission to enable them to move forward (Buck, 2020).

If the new member or senior leader has been promoted from within the school, then the transition is going to mean adjusting the interpersonal relationships that they had previously with middle leaders and staff as well as recalibrating the relationship with pupils. This transition can be assisted by ensuring that the line management responsibilities do not coincide with previous teams they worked with, in as far as is practicable. This will give the space that is needed for those existing relationships to recalibrate to the new reality to which previous professional relationships will need to adapt.

As the new member of senior leadership team settles into their new role where you are looking for them to establish themselves in the wider community as a functional leader, then you should be considering transitioning the relationship that you have with them to a coaching model where you are supporting them to navigate their enhanced role. The key with coaching is that it helps facilitate thinking, and by making the transition into coaching, the coachee will be able to unpack their journey in a safe space where they are able to make sense of the challenges, they face through a learning conversation (Weick, 1995). Connor and Pokora (2017) highlight the importance of developing learning relationships, and for the senior leader to continue to progress, it is key to develop a safe learning relationship to enable them to flourish as a professional learner. Providing high challenge and low threat enables the leader to develop into their role as a professional learner (Myatt, 2016).

When starting to think about wider school issues, and leading change, the coach's role will become imperative, especially when the senior leader needs to lead on key leadership projects. This leadership project will give the senior leader an opportunity to lead system change within a constrained remit so that middle leaders and teachers can see that the leader can deliver a project and build the confidence of wider teams in their changed leadership abilities (Cameron and Green, 2019; Hill, 2002). Having a coach to explore their thinking and ideas in a safe space will help them to develop their confidence to work with their teams in a measured way.

As they start to effect change within a new project or strategic responsibility, this is when the coaching model should be in place specifically to help them to reflect and consider the progress and implications of the change leadership project, but more importantly, as mentioned above, to provide them with a safe opportunity to explore and present their vision, road map with and give ideas to the coach, who will help facilitate the thinking around these issues before it is shared with a team.

Recognising the Scope of the Mentee Role

In the initial phases of the senior leader's journey, as the mentor, you should spend time getting a copy of the job description for the new member of the senior leadership team and discuss with the head teacher the specifics of the mentee's role and remit. Once you have a clear understanding of the responsibilities of your mentee across the school and within the team, you can help them to explore the bounds of their role.

The discussion of the scope of the role and the teams that they will be working with should be the focus of the first mentor meeting with your mentee. This will then help them to understand the daily operational responsibilities that they need to ensure are completed and the capacity they have to complete the rest of the required work each week. However, it is also important to ask mentees how they view the role, what they are hoping to contribute and how their vision and the vision of their line manager needs to be aligned to enable them to lead teams successfully. Giving the senior leader autonomy and agency will make all the difference, as they will feel valued and empowered (Durrant, 2020; Pink, 2018).

Explore with your mentee how meetings will occur with their teams that they lead and the amount of preparation work that will be needed in advance, which will help them to be fully prepared for those key initial meetings where the tone is set.

Recognising Mentee Anxiety and Imposter Syndrome

When your mentee moves into their new role, there will be a number of underlying anxieties that they will be feeling, and these may be bubbling under the surface, but will need addressing in a sensitive way. Browne (2020) highlights that some leaders will suffer from imposter syndrome where they will be concerned that others might feel that they are 'fake' or a 'fraud'. Acknowledging and sharing these anxieties in a supportive manner will help them to settle into their role. At times, talking through the Dreyfus Model (2004) might also help to put the journey in perspective, to have a shared understanding of where the new senior leader is on that journey, and how mentoring and coaching can support.

Common anxieties that are often shared are:

- What if I make a mistake and impact negatively on learners and staff?
- Will my contributions in meetings be listened to by other members of the senior team?
- How do I have difficult conversations with experienced middle leaders who have been in their roles for a long time?

These anxieties could be linked to a feeling that they could be 'found out' that they do not know how to deal with the myriad of situations that will arise for them on a daily basis. As the mentor, the tone which you set during your meetings will decide whether these anxieties are internalized by your mentee or shared. It is important to be aware of negative bias, that the mentee will experience negatives far more intensely and that it is important to celebrate success throughout the journey too (Grenville-Cleave, 2016).

Acknowledging to the mentee that everyone is unsure of themselves when they take on a new role, and it is perfectly natural to feel this way, and if they can share these concerns with you, it would be an effective way in which you can ease those concerns.

The manner in which you approach your mentoring is important and for this you should adopt a reflexive as well as a reflective approach to your mentoring (Door, 2015). A reflexive mentor is one that considers the emotional impact of their approach to mentoring and the impact that it has on all of those involved and must therefore focus on the holistic development of the mentee, and their practice is research and evidence informed, and they don't just focus on the operational aspects of the role.

Mentoring Senior Leaders to Lead Change

Barnett and McCormick (2012) describe the key leadership processes for senior executive leadership teams as:

- Direction setting,
- Managing team operations,
- Developing team leadership capacity.

These are then applied to the teams that they work with to effect change so that the desired outcomes for teams become improved team performance and team effectiveness.

In between these inputs (direction setting, managing team operations and developing team leadership capacity) and the desired outcomes (improved team performance and team effectiveness) are the team processes that the new senior leader will need to work on to effect change. To help shape this process effectively, the leadership coach will play an imperative role.

Barnett and McCormick (2012) identify four distinct processes that enabled teams to develop team leadership capacity, and these will be returned to throughout this chapter:

- Cognitive processes,
- Motivational processes,
- Affective processes,
- Coordination processes.

When supporting a new senior leader to manage and lead the change process with their teams, it is important that they understand the cognitive processes that exist within their teams. Barnett and McCormick define this as:

> Shared knowledge of team members' strengths and weaknesses enabled SLT members to compensate for each other through a shared understanding of team interaction.

Reflective Task

Consider the senior leadership team that the new senior leader has joined, and write down for each one, three key strengths that they exhibit and three areas for development that you know of.

In one of your first mentoring meetings, discuss with your mentee what they consider to be their top three strengths and how these will help the team overall to become more effective. Elicit from your mentee, how they envision supporting their colleagues as well as utilizing their strengths and what they bring to the team. Ask your mentee to identify three areas of their professional experience where they feel they could do with further experience. Framing this in terms of confidence rather than competence will mean that the mentee's defence mechanisms will not be triggered, and you are more likely to gain a truer picture of the key areas that you will be working on with them.

After the meeting, map the strengths that you have across the rest of the team to identify who within the team can help to provide mentoring or coaching for the specific skills or experiences that your mentee has self-identified. The utilisation of coaching to support with the development of specific experience and to build confidence will lead to an increase in role specific competence.

When we then consider the motivational processes within the team and the integration of your mentee within the existing team, you should examine the global motivations of the whole team and then discuss and capture the personal motivations that your mentee has. This will be linked to their values and experiences that have shaped them professionally and personally to this point in their career.

Thinking about the wider team, what are the motivating factors that drive them? How is this linked to the strategic priorities of the school? What are their shared values?

To assist with the integration of the new member of the team, you may want to use as prompt questions to use with the whole team. By going through this process, you will be enabling an ideal opportunity for some peer-mentoring to help the new team member to learn and adopt these shared values.

> ### Reflective Task
>
> While working with the whole team, ask them to discuss and then bring together a single statement which captures the values of what the team believes in.
>
> Next, identify the non-negotiables, the things that are at the core of the vision for the pupils within the school. These are what you will all protect for the educational well-being of the pupils in your care.
>
> Finally, identify the legacy that, as a group, you would like to pass on to all of the pupils within the school.

To help with the integration of your mentee into the senior leadership team, you need to consider the effective processes that will enable this integration and the free flow of ideas between members of the team. How will you enable the 'outsider' to understand and share the unwritten rules of social interaction between the members of the team and for them to navigate these embedded social norms?

Before the first meeting of this established team that your mentee will join, talk them through the social rules of the meeting and what they should expect of the established culture. Explain to them that aspects of the meeting are privileged information, and they should ask if they are unsure of what can be shared with staff that they line manage. The building and maintaining of a shared collective identity as a group will greatly assist their integration into the team.

As your mentee develops a sense of the culture of the leadership team of the organisation that they have joined, the informal checking in and catch-ups with you that you both have in the corridor and around the school will be key to helping them to feel that they are a member of the team.

With your mentee being new to their role, you will have to work with them to navigate the systems now open to them and to understand how to leverage the support that will be needed to effect change within the organisation. With all of these leveraged processes, you will need to talk through with your mentee what the workload implications of each of the levers for the staff involved are and how to balance expediency with achievability of change. These coordination processes need to be managed carefully, and talking through these with your mentee is important if they are going to get support for the work that they need to achieve from the teams that they line manage.

Mentoring Senior Leaders to Work with Their Teams

Supporting your mentee to establish themselves with their existing teams is going to be an ongoing process throughout their first year in post. Each team leader will have their own strengths and areas for development as well as leadership style with which they lead their own team.

For those mentees who are taking on established teams, it would be worth introducing them to the work on situational leadership theory by Hershey and Blanchard (1977), who originated their approach to the leadership of teams in 1969. Beauchamp et al. (2021) might be useful to consider in relation to the importance of adaptive leadership approaches too. This theory has since been developed by both of the original authors, and further information is found within their respective publications. However, the essence of the theory is that, often, leaders need to draw on a repertoire of skills appropriate for the situation to meet the needs of the organisation, learners and tasks (Adiar, 2009). Similar to a mentor and coach's role, in order to be clear on what the needs are of their mentees or coachees and in order to decide how to support in the most suitable way for their needs, leaders need to evaluate and assess how to engage effectively with their context, colleagues, teams and learners. For a novice senior leader, this might take time, and developing their self-awareness of the process and determining how they need to develop as leaders through mentoring and coaching are key to enabling them to develop resilience and the reflective skills and emotional intelligence needed to be effective leaders.

When you are working with your mentee to prepare for their first meeting with their team leaders, take them through the following questions:

- What do we know about the leader of the team? How long have they been working in the school? What are their successes and challenges over the last two years?

- Who is within each of their respective teams? Are there any significant staffing changes that are still settling in?
- What are the goals that this team must achieve from a whole-school level within the next twelve months?
- What recent challenges or turbulence has that the team experienced? What is the typical response of the leader and team to externally imposed turbulence?

Once you have talked through these points with your mentee, ask them to prepare the mentoring questions that they will be using with their team leaders to triangulate the viewpoint of the school with the perceived reality of their team leaders.

Sample questions that they could use with their team leaders are as follows:

- What are the strengths of your team?
- What challenges have you been through in the last twelve months?
- What were the key things that you learnt about your team when they faced this turbulence?
- What do you have to achieve with your team over the next twelve months?
- What do you want to achieve with your team over the next twelve months?
- What can we do to help you and your team achieve these aims?

Work with your mentee to engineer opportunities for you to drop into the working areas of the team and have informal conversations with them. This will give your mentee the chance to triangulate what the team leader is saying about how the team operates with your own sense of what you are learning. An ideal follow-up activity is for your mentee to undertake a joint learning walk with the team leader to discuss what you are seeing.

Mentoring Senior Leaders to Address Difficult Situations

Inevitably the new senior leader will come to you for advice about how to deal with difficult situations that may either arise from an incident directly involving themselves or is passed up to them from one of their teams that they line manage. It is important for your mentee to preserve the autonomy around their decision-making so they can own the outcomes of the decisions that they make. However, along with this they must also enjoy having your support in public as well as in private when they are dealing with complex or difficult decisions.

Let the new senior leader know that your door is always open for a discussion and encourage an open dialogue about situations that arise so that you can provide the opportunity for a coaching conversation, however short, so that they can talk through the issues and come to a course of action. If they are inexperienced in dealing with this type of situation, then providing the opportunity to explore options that you can leverage support for will also be helpful for them. It is often the case that senior leaders will deal with dilemmas, and Steare's (2013) framework is a useful tool to use to help frame the thinking when a school leader encounters an ethical dilemma. Steare outlines key questions to consider:

- What are the Rules?
- Are we acting with Integrity?
- Who is this Good for?
- Who could we Harm?
- What's the Truth? Are we willing to be open, honest and accountable for our actions?

The above questions help you to frame the new leader's thinking in relation to the dilemma, and this model is particularly helpful when considering ethical dilemmas. CollectiveEd (2021) provides a useful dilemma based coaching model which you can draw on in scenarios which are related more to the day-to-day challenges in a school day:

> Starting a conversation about a dilemma:
>
> - Describe the dilemma you are concerned with.
> - Outline the key challenges you are faced with.
> - Who does the dilemma involve?
> - How does it make you feel?
> - What is influencing what is happening right now?
> - What are the opportunities for change?
> - How confident are you at the moment about your knowledge and experience to lead on this dilemma?
> - What are your options at the moment?
> - Who can you approach to support you with this dilemma?
> - Who else can you discuss this with?
> - What other support do you need to address this issue?
> - What are your first steps to move this forward?

Learning through dilemmas:

> - Did you try anything new in relation to this dilemma?
> - What are your learning regarding your team and yourself as a leader as you work through this dilemma?
> - Do you see things differently, and if so, what are your reflections regarding these insights?
> - How might the SLT gain insights through these experiences?

An adaptation of the CollectiveEd Dilemma Based Model (2021).

Providing public support for a decision that the new senior leader has made and then following up with a more detailed coaching conversation is an important learning strategy for the new senior leader. Helping the new senior leader to understand the implications of the course of action that they have taken and then helping them to navigate the fall-out and follow-up work is an important aspect of the mentoring and coaching support that you will be giving them.

Mentoring Senior Leaders to Work Well with Parents and Other Stakeholders

When the new senior leader takes on their first public-facing event as a member of the senior leadership team, it is worth spending time with them during their support meeting to talk them through the key messages that need to be communicated, either verbally or through their presence.

As a member of the senior leadership team, they are part of the corporate face of the school or organization, and as such they are under scrutiny by everyone at the event, whether it is their first assembly, parents' evening or public event. The staff will be looking for how they circulate, talk to the staff present and engage with pupils and with members of the public. As a brand ambassador, they are communicating the values and expectations that the whole leadership team are judged by (Buck, 2016; Browne, 2020). Members of the leadership team should be on hand to support teachers during open events as a passive, but visible, presence only becoming involved when they are needed.

Getting this balance right is something that you will need to discuss with your mentee in advance of each of their 'firsts', whether that is a whole school assembly or prize-giving. Giving them the opportunity to shadow you on one of these events so that you can model the expected behaviours and interactions will help the new senior leader to emulate this in future.

The follow-up discussion at the end of the event to help the new senior leader to reflect on how they found the event will consolidate their learning and help them to take the next step independently.

Mentoring Senior Leaders to Work Effectively with School Governors or Trustees

Another important stakeholder group that the new senior leader will need to navigate and forge a relationship with are school governors or trustees. As a new member of the senior leadership team, the new senior leader may have limited contact with governors or trustees at the early stages of their journey, but helping them to manage this relationship is important because it will reflect on the rest of the senior team. Useful texts to work through with the new senior leader might be the Department for Education's (2020) *Governance Handbook and Competency Framework*. This is a useful document to outline to the new senior leader what the strategic role of the governing board is. You can also ask your new senior leader to look at the school's own handbook on governance and its policies regarding governance. You can follow this up with a further conversation on what governance means in relation to the senior leader's role within the school and who their link governor is that they will be working with more closely.

If the new senior leader has a specific area of responsibility that falls under the remit of a link governor or trustee, you will need to talk the new leader through the specific bounds of the relationship that they will be entering into. A structured discussion with the new leader about the role of any liaison meeting or visit by a governor or trustee will enable them to prepare in advance with information that is pertinent and helpful so that the meeting is productive to both parties.

Building and maintaining strong working relationships between the senior team and the governors or trustees will be the bedrock of supporting the long-term development of the school, and so getting it right from the start is crucial for new members of the senior team.

Facilitating Thinking

Within the busy professional life of the senior leader, you should help them to find time and the mental headspace to pause and reflect on their work and role. Encouraging them to be critically reflective of what is working well and what they need to perhaps do differently is key to helping them to process their own learning journey as a new member of the senior team.

It is important to remember that being critically reflective is not the same as being self-critical (Door, 2015). Critical reflection is the process of mentally digesting something that has made you stop and think and of formulating a course of action as a result of that reflective thought. This is a positive process that helps to formulate learned courses of action because you have reflected on your experiences. In this way you are then developing a professional schema that you can build upon through further experiences, thus deepening this professional schema with each experience that is analysed through this process of critical reflection.

As the mentor or coach, how are you going to ensure that your mentee has this opportunity to critically reflect on their professional experience regularly? This could be done through your regular mentoring or coaching meetings, or you could encourage your mentee to keep a reflective diary or journal into which they commit just the critical incidents, their reflection and what their course of action would be if that incident happened again.

If the school is large enough that there are multiple people holding the same role, it may be possible to set up a regular session either formally or informally for the assistant head teachers, for example, to get together themselves and to discuss their week and to critically reflect on their learning.

Where the mentee is within a school that is part of a Multi-Academy Trust, there may be some opportunities to facilitate this across schools, but the mentor needs to reflect on whether the same level of honest critical self-reflection would be achieved with someone from outside of the school.

Well-Being – What Does It Mean in the Context of Senior Leadership?

As your mentee or coachee has stepped up into a senior leadership role, their terms and conditions of employment have now fundamentally changed, which, if they are not careful, effects an open-ended expectation on their time and mental energies. When the new senior leader makes this change, you will need to be mindful of the implicit and explicit demands that you put on their time as well as the amount of work that they take on with their own teaching commitments and the strategic responsibilities that they now have.

Here is where the pervading culture within the school leadership team plays a very influential part in the approach to managing the well-being and welfare of the staff.

Ask yourself the following questions:

- When are members of the leadership team expected to be in school and why?
- When do members of the leadership team go home?
- Who is contactable outside of 'normal' school hours and why?
- When are people expected to switch off from school?
- Which members of the team are expected to be at school events? What is the rationale, and how are these distributed between the team?

These may seem like benign questions, but they do enable you to reflect on the culture that exists within the school that your mentee is joining.

Do members of the senior team have time and communication boundaries in place? The pervasiveness of social media tools within school leadership teams now means that communication between senior team members and the implicit expectation of being able to respond to these messages is a double-edged sword. As the mentor, ask yourself the following:

- When should your new senior leader be able to switch off from the social media tools that we use?
- When should the new senior leader switch off their email?
- What is a reasonable expectation of when emails could be replied to?
- What constitutes an emergency? How should I contact the new senior leader?

The school will, of course, have an out of hours emergency procedure that will be operable under certain circumstances, and this will need to be discussed with the new senior leader. Their role within it and the conditions on which they will cascade messages down to their team leaders needs to be explicitly discussed.

Once you have reflected on these questions, you can then have a discussion with the new senior leader about the time boundaries within which they are expected to operate as a member of the team and when is their own personal time.

Your own reflection on the answers to these questions may prompt a wider discussion amongst the Senior team about how you maintain your own work-life balance.

Helping the Career Development of Your Mentee

Once you have helped the new senior leader to establish the operational aspects of their role, you can then start turning to the strategic aspects of their role and support them in broadening their experience ready for future potential promotions.

A healthy organization is always looking to develop the leadership capacity of their staff, even if that means promotion to other schools. The regular turnover of staff so that they can gain promotion is a healthy indicator of the ethos of the school in that they believe in the development and fulfilment of the untapped potential of their staff.

Within their role descriptor, the new senior leader will have specific strategic responsibilities, and through your mentoring and coaching support, they will grow into these, but you should also discuss with them where their career aspirations lie.

Broadening experience across the range of strategic responsibilities within the team is a good place to start and, this can be facilitated through rotating responsibilities between staff at the same level, for example, assistant headteacher, every couple of years. When this is combined with specific negotiated additional developmental projects that can be completed within an academic year, these developmental activities will enable the new senior leader to start building the range of experiences that they will need when applying for promotion, either internally or externally.

To help frame the mentoring or coaching conversation around career development, here are some prompt questions that you may want to use:

- What are the aspects of your current role that you are enjoying and want to deepen your knowledge or experience of?
- Considering the challenges that the school faces, how do you think we could develop further capacity to face this challenge more confidently?
- If you could swap one of your strategic responsibilities with another member of the team, which one would it be and why?
- Where do you see the gaps in your professional experience that we could help you to fill?
- What are your career aspirations, and what can we do to help you achieve them?

The decision by you as the mentor or coach to support the new senior leader to chart out their future career pathway will show the values that your school lives through the way in which they support the aspirations of their own staff. Providing opportunities for career development will also help to retain these senior members of staff within your school as they will see that you are invested in them as individuals and they will only choose to move on when they are ready for their next step, rather than moving on much quicker because they are unsatisfied in their role. The management of talent within your organisation is key to enhancing the reputation of the school as a good place to work, which will in turn help to attract future talent to apply for roles when they are advertised. As the mentor, you have a key role in this talent management programme within the school.

The decision by you as the mentor or coach to support the new senior leader to chart out their future career pathway will show the values that your school lives through the way in which they support the aspirations of their own staff. Providing opportunities for career development will also help to retain these senior members of staff within your school as they will see that you are invested in them as individuals, and they will only choose to move on when they are ready for their next step, rather than moving on much quicker because they are unsatisfied in their role. The management of talent within your organization is key to enhancing the reputation of the school as a good place to work, which will in turn help to attract future talent to apply for roles when they are advertised. As the mentor, you have a key role in this talent management programme within the school.

Case Studies

In this case study on coaching aspiring women leaders, Sarah Mullin illustrates that as the mentor or coach, you have a key role in helping to unearth the potential in the colleagues that you mentor or coach and to always be alert to the possibility of helping others.

As a coach, I view my role as enabling women to dig deep within to unearth their potential so that they feel empowered to achieve their personal and professional goals. Participants are invited to reflect on their previous experiences, considering ways that they have led in different contexts, so that they can identify and articulate the skills and attributes they possess. From here, women are encouraged to consider how they might enhance their leadership styles and strengths, proactively seeking ways to develop their skillset by creating opportunities which adequately prepare them to navigate the journey to school leadership.

Many of the women I have supported through coaching have become the middle leaders and senior leaders they have long aspired to be. There have been women who felt they had been overlooked for positions they believed were just right for them; there have been women who might have otherwise been lost to the profession as they struggled to balance their personal and professional responsibilities; there have been women who I saw had so much potential, yet they found themselves working in an environment where their talents were not being nurtured.

There is nothing better than receiving a call or an email from someone I have coached to success. I am proud to lead by example, and it is such an honour to hear that I have inspired others to start a doctorate in education degree or begin writing a book. I love it when another woman feels that she will also pursue her career goals whilst also raising a family. It makes me so proud to know that, as a coach for aspiring women leaders, I am playing a small part in driving social change, helping to promote equality and diversity in educational leadership. It is a privilege to know that the impact of coaching has enabled my women participants to see themselves the way that I have seen them right from our very first session: as future changemakers.

A key message shared with all of my coaching participants is that as women shatter glass ceilings, it is important that we reach out and help other women who are walking the same paths we once trod. Empowered women empower women. Of course, it is wonderful to see coaching participants achieve their individual career success, but I believe it is our moral duty to inspire women to support one another, working collaboratively and providing opportunities which enable other women to thrive. By shining a light on the talents of another woman, we have the ability to support that woman in seeing her own worth.

As a coach, it is fantastic to be able to help women to become ethical leaders who lead with integrity, honesty and respect. We have the opportunity to create the leaders we wished we had worked with and that we want the next generation to see in action. By empowering other women to succeed as leaders, we have the opportunity to gain momentum, championing one another and serving as positive role models for children and young women so that they can see the many benefits of equity and diversity in school leadership. The power of coaching is phenomenal. Collectively, we have the opportunity to change leadership narrative for generations to come.

This case study from Maria French illustrates the power of mentoring specific skills and the legacy effect that this can have in helping a colleague to grow in confidence so that they can grow into their role within the school.

Inspiration: The inspiration came from a leadership project that I completed with The Princes' Teaching Institute, entitled *Find Your Voice!* A three-year research project looking into the impact of teaching girls how to speak in public. The offshoot was the realization that the teachers needed support to develop the confidence and skills to deliver assemblies and speak in public, so in turn they could model this and offer more opportunities for students to co-plan and deliver a whole school assembly. The joy and privilege of coaching and mentoring a colleague to deliver their first assembly is essential. For me, this is where the magic happens in school and where you evangelize your ethos and culture.

Impact: The impact of this type of coaching and mentoring can really transform a school. It also grows its own momentum and flair. Delivering an assembly, particularly in a large secondary school, can be too daunting for some teachers and this might hold them back in their careers or in what they want to achieve. Coaching for assemblies is built on trust, as the risk factor is high. Great assemblies inspire awe and wonder- what a gift and worth investing the time in! Consideration of the content and vision for their first assembly starts with vocal and breathing exercises. Is a microphone needed, and how does this affect your ability to move in the space? The detail is key, and all teachers should know how to use a microphone professionally – this models it as the norm for the young audience and takes away their fear. I support staff to be able to do everything themselves tech-wise so that if you are in front of 400 students and there is a technical glitch, you can troubleshoot yourself. Timing, tempo, pace, whether to use humour or not and how the assembly lands, knowing your audience and re-imagining what is of interest for an assembly, are a few of the considerations in this mentoring. However, the biggest impact of this specific coaching and mentoring is building confidence in teachers. Bucket loads of encouragement is required. It is all worth it when at the end you stand at the back of a packed assembly hall and young people break into applause for an awesome and inspirational assembly – you know that the teacher has a new skill in their arsenal that will take them places.

Legacy

Hopefully, colleagues will pass that gift on – so that the power and gift of school assemblies continues to develop and grow. Encouraging our students to stand with us on stage and be part of the assembly – and not read from paper – but talk with passion and confidence about their message is the icing on the cake. There are so many issues that young people want to hear more about – want to be participate in the conversation about – issues that really make them sit up and listen, that the future of school assemblies is top of my list for post-pandemic school.

The legacy of time spent coaching a colleague to become proficient and readily confident to deliver a whole school assembly has enormous impact. It raises their profile within the school, as well as offers our young people another role model in effective communication and a teacher who will support them to be part of an assembly. What started as a project with the PTI has become a staff development option too and one that can eradicate the nerves and empower our teachers to stand with confidence in front of their colleagues, as well as the occasional tough crowd of teenagers, to really inspire awe and wonder – what a gift!

Reflective Task

1. How could imposter syndrome present itself in your mentee? What approaches would you take to put them at ease and support them?
2. What career development opportunities are available within your school for newly appointed members of the senior leadership team?
3. How do you model maintaining a healthy work-life balance for the new senior leader?

Recommended Reading

Atwal, K. (2019), *The Thinking School: Developing a Dynamic Learning Community*. UK: John Catt Education Ltd.

Blanchard, K., Fowler, S. and Hawkins, L. (2018), *Self-Leadership and the One Minute Manager, Gain the Mindset and Skillset for Getting What You Need to Succeed*. London: Harper Thorsons.

Campbell, J. and van Nieuwerburgh, C. (2018), *The Leader's Guide to Coaching in Schools: Creating Conditions for Effective Learning*. UK: Corwin.

Durrant, J. (2020), *Teacher Agency, Professional Development and School Improvement*. Oxon: Routledge.

Harris et al. (2003), Effective Leadership for School Improvement: Routledge Falmer.

Kerry, T. (2005), Mastering Deputy Headship: Acquiring the Skills for Future Leadership.

References

Adair, J. (2009), *The Inspirational Leader: How to Motivate, Encourage and Achieve Success* (The John Adair Leadership Library), UK: Kogan Page.

Barnett, K. and McCormick, J. (2012) 'Leadership and Team Dynamics in Senior Executive Leadership Teams', *Educational Management Administration & Leadership*, 40(6), pp. 653–71. doi: 10.1177/1741143212456909.

Beauchamp, G., Hulme, M, Clarke, L. Hamilton, L. and Harvey, J. A. (2021), 'People miss people': A study of school leadership and management in the four nations of the United Kingdom in the early stage of the COVID-19 pandemic, Educational Management Administration & Leadership, 1–18 Available at: Beauchamp et al. 2021 people miss people (1).pdf (Accessed: 04. 01.2021).

Blanchard, K., Fowler, S. and Hawkins, L. (2018), *Self-Leadership and the One Minute Manager, Gain the Mindset and Skillset for Getting What You Need to Succeed*. London: Harper Thorsons.

Browne, A. (2020), *Light the Way: The Case for Ethical Leadership in Schools*. UK: Bloomsbury.

Buck, A. (2016), *Leadership Matters*. UK: John Catt Publication.

Buck, A. (2020), *The BASIC Coaching Method: All You Need to Know to Coach with Confidence*. UK: Cadogan Press.

Cameron, E. and Green, M. (2019), *Making Sense of Change Management: A Complete Guide to the Models, Tools, and Techniques of Organisational Change*, 5th edn. London: Kogan Page.

Connor, M. and Pokora, J. (2017), *Coaching and Mentoring at Work: Developing Effective Practice*, 3rd edn. London: Open University Press.

DfE (1995), *Guidance: The Seven Principles of Public Life*. London: Department for Education. Available: The Seven Principles of Public Life - GOV.UK (www.gov.uk) (Accessed: 01.06.2021).

DfE (2020), Governance handbook and competency framework, UK: DfE. Available at: https://www.gov.uk/government/publications/governance-handbook (Accessed: 01.06.2021).

Door, V. (2015), *Developing Creative and Critical Educational Practitioners*. UK: Critical Publishing.

Dreyfus, S. (2004), 'The five-stage model of adult skill acquisition, bulletin of science'. *Technology & Society*, 24(3), June 2004, pp. 177–81, Available: Dreyfus-skill-level.pdf (bu.edu) (Accessed: 01. 06.2021).

Grenville-Cleave, B. (2016), *Positive Psychology: A Toolkit for Happiness, Purpose and Well-Being*. UK: Icon Books Ltd.

Hersey, P. and Blanchard, K. H. (1977), *Management of Organizational Behavior 3rd Edition– Utilizing Human Resources*. New Jersey: Prentice Hall.

Hill, M. (2002), *School Leadership and Complex Theory*. UK: Routledge.

Lane, G. and Clutterbuck, D. (2005), *Situational Mentoring: An International Review of Competences and Capabilities in Mentoring*. UK: Sage.

Lofthouse, R. (2021), *Dilemma Based Coaching*. UK: CollectiveEd.

Myatt, M. (2016), *High Challenge Low Risk*. UK: John Catt Publishing.
Pink, D. (2018), *Drive: The Surprising Truth about What Motivates Us*. UK: Canongate Books.
Steare, R. (2013), *Ethicability: How to Decide What's Right and Find the Courage to Do*. USA: Roger Steare Consulting Limited.
Weick, K. (1995), *Sensemaking in Organisations*. London: Sage.

7

Mentoring and Coaching Headteachers

Derek Boyle and Lizana Oberholzer

Aims and Objectives

In this chapter we will be exploring approaches that can be used to mentor people that are taking on a head of school or head teacher type role. This may be within a stand-alone school or within a Multi-Academy Trust, and each of these will have their own challenges for both the mentee/coachee and mentor/coach as they will have different professional dynamics that will need to be recognized and reconciled.

As a headteacher, your mentee or coachee, depending on their needs, will be the visible corporate face of the school, and they will have to navigate a myriad of different relationships and the legacy of their predecessor as they begin to make the case for and implement new changes.

This chapter therefore aims to:

- Develop a clear understanding of how headteachers can be supported through the use of mentoring and coaching,
- Explore approaches and practices that support headteachers through mentoring and coaching,
- Suggest ways to enable headteachers to effectively make the case for change by communicating their vision well to a variety of stakeholders,
- Show how headteachers can be mentored to lead change while also balancing and managing their stakeholders.

Introduction

Mentoring or coaching a new headteacher or head of a school is a role that will require sensitivity and patience, as the new principal leader of the school will be establishing themselves both within their own school, with your support, and also within the local community of principal leaders of schools within their local area. The politics and rivalry between schools within the local authority area are complicated, and establishing yourself within this external group is an added level of complexity to the mentoring relationship. One of the principal roles of the mentor or coach will be to help the new leader to navigate the landscape and to make sense of these complex systems and issues they will encounter (Weick, 1995).

In this chapter the term 'principal teacher' will be used to encompass the roles of both the headteacher of a stand-alone school and the head of school role for someone operating within a Multi-Academy Trust (MAT).

If the new principal teacher is going to flourish within their new role, they will need a mentor or coach who can also be a critical friend, who can provide a 'listening ear' as well as constructive advice (Skinner and Oberholzer, 2020).

Making the Case for Change

When the new headteacher applied for and was interviewed for the role that they now hold, they articulated their vision for the school under their stewardship. However, as Pain (2019) outlines, this vision also needs to align with a vision for the organisation that is in line with the view of the trustee board or the governing board. It is important for your mentee to appreciate that the school has existing values and traditions which they will need to engage with, understand and be taking responsibility for when deciding on the pace and appropriateness of any change that they wish to make. They will be leading a distributed community that is either currently attached to the school or have links to the school through their children or through having worked their themselves.

Helping the new headteacher to articulate the vision that they have, align it to the governor's or trustee board's vision and to recognize the pace of the change that they want to make is key to helping them to put at ease those currently within the school and under their leadership. As discussed in Chapter 6, it is also important to explore the Nolan Principals of public life (DfE, 1995) and ensure that the leader has a clear understanding of the importance of the expectations and the school's value set. Working through the Association or School and College Leader's (ASCL) Ethical framework (2020) is important too, to outline the expectations, as well as the Headteacher's Standards (DfE, 2020). In addition, it is important to continue to explore how the headteacher can be true to themselves and align their own values with that of their school, and lead with authenticity and conviction.

To help frame these discussions you could use the following prompt questions:

- What are the current strengths of the school? Can you summarize these in fifty words?
- What did you recognize as the challenges that the school faces during your application and interview process?
- What further information do you need about the school?
- Who can provide that information?
- What capacity is there for change within the school?
- What do you think must be done now and what can wait for a year?
- What do you want to keep and what do you want to change within the school?
- What is the case for change?

Working through these questions with your mentee will help them to synthesize and consolidate their key ideas and thoughts that will become the rationale for any change that they wish to bring. It is imperative that they are clear on the 'why' of the change they wish to lead (Sinek, 2011). This will help them to be able to articulate their vision and the rationale for it more clearly. It might also be worth helping your mentee to prepare their approach to articulating their vision with the trustee board or governing board to ensure that their views align effectively with the board and their strategic vision for the organisation (Pain, 2019). Understanding the strategic function of the board is key in ensuring that the new headteacher can navigate the key aspects of their role effectively.

All new leaders will want to articulate the organisation's vision and to consolidate the mechanisms for implementing that change first within their senior team and then with the wider staff.

As a follow-up exercise, set the new headteacher the following questions to consider and to bring to a future meeting:

- Articulate the strengths of the school within 100 words.
- What are your own personal educational values?
- What do you want to support the school to continue to do?
- What do you see as the immediate challenges for the school?
- What are the longer-term challenges for the school?

Communicating the Vision

Once the new headteacher has worked through and developed answers to making the case for change, you should work with them on how they will communicate their views to all stakeholders, including the trustee or governing board and the different audiences that they represent their views to.

For each of the following stakeholder groups, what are the key points that they will need to get across in language that is accessible to the audience?

- Pupils
- Parents and carers
- Staff
- Volunteers
- Governors or trustees
- The wider community around the school

Short, easily digestible messaging is the key here, especially when conveying key ideas, as well as the rationale for changes, if there are changes being planned (Adair, 2009). A simple, positive rationale for any changes in clear messaging that is unambiguous will be key to getting these messages across and understood. Simply explaining what each of your stakeholder groups can do to support this vision is a useful way in which you can get them invested with the vision that is shared with them (Buck, 2016). If this is linked from what they can continue to do, and then extended to what the change requires them to do more of or do differently, it gives them a platform from which they can understand how the changes will impact on them and the way in which they will work.

What is vital is making the 'why' clear and what the underpinning reasons are for the desired change (Sinek, 2011). Explore with the new headteacher how they need to present the 'why' first, and then progress to 'how' and 'what', as outlined by Sinek (2011). Working through these crucial steps will enable the new leader to reflect on the key components, how the message is received and how they need to consider the potential reaction to the proposed change. It is important to not confuse the leadership theory with the coaching practices and approaches. The purpose of the exercise is to explore the purpose of the leader's direction of travel, and they need to unpack that purpose and the vision clearly; however, as a mentor and coach you need to help frame this thinking process by ensuring that the coachee/mentee is in a calm limbic state. It is often best to unpack the thinking through the use of how and what questions – ask the leader to describe their thinking, what underpins the thinking and how will it help to make the 'why' clearer for example, and convey the purpose clearly. In this way, you will ensure that the leader can reflect and make sense of their learning in a safe reflective space and not become defensive. Thomson (2013) points out that it is important to hold the conversation through what and how questions to enable the coachee to explore their thinking in a supportive and safe way.

Helping the leader to focus their vision and purpose for the organisation is key. Combining the key messages with visual reminders and taking away information that can be revisited will help with embedding the rationale for the changes that the team can expect. Bird and Gornall (2016) point out how using diagrams and asking the leader to map out their thinking can help them to strategize effectively, through seeing their vision starting to shape in a visual way.

Mentoring or Coaching Headteachers to Lead Change

As part of the handover from the previous headteacher, your mentee should have been given an idea of the typical calendar of commitments and strategic decision making that needs to happen in order for the school to function smoothly and for 'leadership' to be seen. Some headteachers are very generous with their time to ensure that their successors are well supported on the journey, but others might be less supportive; practice varies. If you have an opportunity to mentor the new leader before they are in post, when they visit the school prior to the start of their new role, your conversations can centre on what questions to ask and how to obtain the key information they need, such as the school development plan, reports to governors and data, to ensure that the new headteacher can make a flying start (Berry, 2016).

It is also important to agree with the new headteacher how the learning conversations will take place. Some headteachers might be brand new to the role, whereas others are new to the school but are experienced headteachers, and it is key to be clear on what their needs are. For more experienced colleagues, a coaching approach might be more suitable, whereas for a novice headteacher, a mentoring approach might be best placed. Contract and identify key slots when meetings can take place. During the meetings, you can map out on a half-termly and then weekly basis what must be planned for and completed over the course of a typical academic year within the school. These areas may typically include:

- Senior leadership team weekly meeting agendas and minute taking,
- Duty rotas and team meetings associated with them,
- Self-evaluation and improvement planning processes,
- Improvement plan review, setting and monitoring for middle leader teams,
- Appraisal or performance management, meetings and pay committee meetings,

- Governor or trustee meetings,
- Regular meetings with the chair of governors or trustees and the clerk to the governors,
- Budget monitoring,
- Recruitment and transition processes for incoming students,
- School governance processes for the different committees,
- The School Inset and CPD calendar,
- Parents' Evenings,
- School Open evenings and any other commitments.

Preparing themselves for each of these areas is going to need foresight and talking around any issues that might arise, so it is worth keeping the overview plan of the year with you for the meetings with the new leader to remind yourself of what they are currently dealing with.

Once the new leader has got a feel for the organisation and the annual cycle of the school calendar, then they will consider what needs to change immediately, and over the longer term, to align the school more closely with the vision agreed with the governors or trustees that appointed them to the role.

It is worth asking your mentee to go through the vision for the school with you again, the case for change and to ask the following questions of them:

- For this aspect, what is the case for change?
- How will it improve the functioning of the school community and the education of the pupils in your care?
- What must stay the same and why?
- What do you feel must change and why?
- Who will lead the change process?
- Who will enact the change process?
- Who will be impacted by the change process?
- For each group that will lead, enact or will be impacted by the change process, has the rationale for change been explained?
- How will you know that the change has been successful?
- How will the turbulence caused by the change be mitigated?

Having a clearly rationalized case for change and planning for the management of that change will be important for reducing the intentional turbulence caused by the change process (Beabout, 2012). If, on balance, the benefits of the change do not outweigh the turbulence, you should steer your mentee back to asking how the benefits will outweigh the turbulence caused by the change.

Poorly managed change processes can lead to negative impacts on the staff involved as they will be the ones that will be communicating the rationale for change to the other stakeholders involved, such as pupils, parents, and other colleagues. Without a clearly communicated cost-benefit explanation, the change process will be failing while it is being implemented (Adair, 2009; Cameron and Green, 2019). The perception that this change is just for the new headteacher to 'make their mark' on the school without any easily understood benefit for the turbulence created is going to impact on the retention of staff ultimately through frustration and uncertainty (Beabout, 2012).

Managing Stakeholders

When the new headteacher is establishing themselves within the school community, they will need to plan for how they will purposely engage with two distinct groups of stakeholders that have been split into a primary group and a secondary group.

The primary group are those who will be most directly impacted on a daily basis by the leadership and management approach of the new leader and will need constant attention.

The secondary group are those stakeholders that need to be managed and given attention, but these require a more nuanced approach that needs nurturing overtime (Fullan, 2020).

Stakeholders under Primary Grouping

- Pupils,
- Parents or carers,
- Support staff,
- Teaching staff,
- Middle leadership team members,
- Senior leadership team members,
- MAT Chief Executive Officer (CEO),
- Governing or trustee Board.

Ask the new leader to reflect on and consider a response to the following questions for each stakeholder group:

- What are their needs?
- How can I help to meet these needs?
- What are their primary motivations with respect to the school community?
- What are their aspirations?
- What can I do as a leader to help them flourish?

The secondary group are considered groups as they have an 'identity' that needs understanding and exploring how the school will be interacting with them over the longer term. The managing of these relationships can be time-consuming at times but establishing productive relationships with these are going to be linked to both the brand identity of the school and your mentees.

Stakeholders under Secondary Grouping

- Local community,
- Social media,
- Print media,
- Local reputation in the historical context,
- Traditional context of the school within the local family of schools.

For this secondary grouping, the new headteacher should be considering the following:

- What is the existing relationship of the school and the headteacher with this 'group'?
- What key messages need to be maintained, and what new ones need to be established with each group?
- How many resources need to be assigned from across the school to manage this stakeholder 'group'?

On a holistic level, the brand management of the school and of the headteacher is going to have wide-ranging impacts, primarily on recruitment of pupils to the school at entry points but secondly on the recruitment and retention of talent to and within the school. So, investment in this secondary grouping is going to be as important as the primary group for the brand management of the school and the long-term financial viability of the school finances.

Coaching and Mentoring Conversation Topics

Key coaching and mentoring conversations need to centre on the following topics to help the new headteacher to make sense of the complex systems and the educational landscape they need to navigate for their school (Weick, 1995; Hill, 2005):

Coaching and Mentoring Headteachers to Reflect on the Curriculum Provided

- National policy context, including personal values and your personal view of the role of education,
- What is affordable verses what is desirable?

Coaching and Mentoring Headteachers to Reflect on Working Effectively with School Budgets

- Managing financial probity,
- Ethical decision making,
- Managing financial arrangements with MATs.

Coaching and Mentoring Headteachers Dealing with Human Resource Issues

- Human Resource issues – who is the external source of advice?
- Managing the relationship with Unions.

Coaching and Mentoring Headteachers Dealing with Challenging Issues (Parents, Pupils)

- Being true to your values,
- Decompression for headteachers, or well-being,
- Being the ultimate authority,
- Managing the relationship with governors or trustees.

Coaching and Mentoring Headteachers Dealing with Challenging Outcomes and Ofsted

- What can you control?
- Picking yourself and your team up,
- The human touch,
- The importance of safeguarding,
- The importance of risk assessment,
- Role of Academy Improvement Partners and CEO – providing backup for the headteacher and providing support to confirm their conviction.

Coaching and Mentoring Headteachers with Their Career Development Plans

- Where do you want the new headteacher to be in three years' time?
- Giving them time to find their feet,
- Developing roles within a MAT,
- Nurturing talent.

Facilitate Thinking

When supporting a new headteacher as a mentor or coach, you are going to be helping them to navigate the immediate demands of the daily role and the longer-term strategic needs of the school with their vision for the school community that they serve. At times you will need to prompt their thoughts and enable that critical self-reflection, while at other times you will just need to be the listening ear and critical friend while they unpack their thinking (Door, 2015; Skinner and Oberholzer, 2020).

Does the new leader have their own 'leadership time' ring-fenced within their diary each week within which they have the time and mental space to pause and think? When will they be able to take a step away from the business of the day and the constant demands on their attention? In order to ensure that the new leader has this leadership time, they will need to ensure that there is both the capacity within their own senior leadership team to manage the operational aspects of the running of the school and the trusted autonomy to make rationalize decisions that they know that the new headteacher will support. How does your mentee utilize this leadership time? Do they put a 'do not disturb' sign on the door, walk the site or take time away from the school site for a few hours each week?

When working with the new headteacher, ask them to reflect on the following:

1. If you were not in school tomorrow and not contactable, who would ensure that the school still functioned?
2. Is your prolonged absence from employment within the critical incident plan?
3. What does your mentee do within their leadership time?

The Importance of Reflecting on Well-Being and Workload as You Lead Your School

Who looks after the welfare and well-being of the headteacher? Being at the head of the organisation can be a lonely place, so who is looking after them?

Within local authority areas, there is generally a local headteachers' forum that meets regularly to share concerns, receive updates and form a cohesive response to challenges that face all of those present. These forums can provide a ready network of support, but with any organisation (either formal or informal) there is always politics, clichés and agendas to be navigated that can in themselves be draining and frustrating.

Ask your mentee how they switch off when away from the school site and how they achieve the division between personal and professional life? It is important for new headteachers, especially, to realize that they are part of a team within their school and that they do not need to be in charge and on point all of the time. If they insist on micro-managing or being involved with every aspect of every facet of the organisation, they will exhaust themselves quickly. More importantly than this, they will also be preventing their senior team from growing into their roles and developing themselves. A side-effect of this is a paralysis of the decision-making process within the senior team if they feel that the operational details of every aspect needs to be run by the headteacher first. The senior team needs to feel that they have earned autonomy in decision-making and just the high-level details may need confirming with the headteacher prior to commencement of a new project.

At times, your mentee will feel the pressure building, so it is at these critical times that you as the mentor should be asking them to reflect on why they love the job that they do. Working from the assumption that they enjoy the job forces the mentee to reflect on their core values and their inner drive that provides their passion for the role.

Reminding them to take regular walks around the school to interact with the pupils in their care, the staff that they work alongside and the parents or carers that trust the education of their children to the headteacher is an important way of reconnecting with their inner drive and reminds them about why they love the job that they do.

Case Study 1

Within this case study, Jill Berry explains the personal value that having a good mentor or coach has, not just for the person that you are mentoring. This can also have a ripple effect for future generations of headteachers.

Outline:
I have been coaching and mentoring aspiring and serving headteachers since I stepped down from headship in 2010. It has been a pleasure and a privilege to support a number of heads as they embark on and then move forward in the role. I strongly believe that being the headteacher is the best job in a school – I certainly found my own headship to be the most fulfilling and joyful of the seven jobs I had across my thirty-year career. But school leadership is not without its challenges, and having a supportive, committed and empathetic coach or mentor with whom you can discuss frankly and openly, and in complete confidence, what you are dealing with and how best you can navigate it can make all the difference to how you feel about your role and what you accomplish in it.

Impact:
The coaching and mentoring sessions I have led with headteachers have been both face-to-face and online, and sometimes over the telephone. The heads I have worked with have told me that just having the opportunity to talk to someone who has set aside the time to listen, reflect and respond can bring a sense of release and relief. It is helpful if the coach or mentor is external to the organisation you work within and someone who understands the pressures and the rewards of headship.

As a mentor I will sometimes say, 'Have you thought about ...?' or 'Could it be worth trying to ...?', but the heads know that the decisions about where to go next and what to do are always theirs. Talking it through can, they tell me, help them to clarify their thinking and their resolve. Sometimes the conversation serves to remind them of progress they have made and work they are proud of, and this can help them to feel better about themselves and to increase their self-belief.

I send out a bullet point summary of what we have discussed after each session, and, over time, revisiting the record of earlier conversations can increase the head's sense that they are continuing to learn and to develop their skills and their confidence.

Legacy:
The heads benefiting from coaching and mentoring support now are likely to be the ones who are offering coaching and mentoring to future generations of

school leaders, 'paying it forward', and bolstering and constructively challenging the cohorts of headteachers who will follow them, guiding and counselling them to become their professional best. And as a coach or a mentor you have a valuable opportunity to reflect and to continue to learn yourself, which is satisfying and gives you a strong sense of purpose.

We need to continue to invest in the development of leaders at all levels in all types of organisations, and the role of coach and mentor is integral to this investment. Coaching and mentoring build capacity, confidence and collective efficacy. It is a privilege to be part of this. As Wigston (2021) says in 'The Magic in the Space Between', 'The intimacy of being listened to; the space and time to explore and discuss; the opportunity to put themselves first for a change – it is these aspects of mentoring that have helped mentees on our programme to, in the words of St Thomas, 'bring forth what is within you'.

Jill Berry is a former head, a leadership development consultant and the author of Making the Leap – Moving from Deputy to Head (*Crown House, 2016*).

Case Study 2

In this case study, Dr Matt Silver explains the legacy effect of a long-term commitment to the coaching and development of staff within the leadership team, based on shared values and strengthening the culture of support and challenge.

Set in a secondary Special Education Needs (SEND) setting in London, the use of coaching, in particular the values assessment, developed over twenty-five years of executive business coaching by Complete. The aim was to support the vertical development of the leadership team, providing a map for the individual, the collective and the strategy. This developed the values of the outcomes of education and, by integrating them, found a very positive impact across all stakeholders and beyond the school gates. Delivery was mixed between half-termly, whole team and individual external delivery, and day-to-day and weekly routines, rituals and practices for coaching presence both formally and in the culture.

The leadership team became conscious of where they were developmentally in the values profile, mapped against Graves (1970) and Beck and Cowan's (1990) spiral dynamics work. Of course, the lines of development were subject to the individual and the stage they were at upon that line. Coaching, the common vocabulary and their own step change in their development saw them transcend and include the strength of each stage whilst addressing their shadows of prior stages, using them as leverage to motivate the deep work. The impact saw results triple in a SEND setting; behaviour challenges reduced by 83 per cent, staff absence reduced by 43 per cent and the budget income increased by £250,000 per year. The team development index shifted, individual leaders felt transformed and the organisation became deliberately developmental. The repeat of the values assessment eighteen months later saw significant shifts in values stages that were reflected in observed behaviour by the coachee and the coach.

The culture of the organisation. While schools are largely focused on learning and learning outcomes, bringing the concept of vertical development has changed the paradigm around the outcomes of the system, what is possible and how they can be measured. Drip-feeding this through individual growth and then into the culture has allowed for psychological safety to improve, higher well-being and the value that this and our integrated lines of development brought into the curriculum, enhancing academic outcomes without being purely focused on them.

An understanding of these maps and it being baked into culture through rituals, practices and language has allowed succession planning to be in operation and for future leaders and staff being willing to peer coach and lean into the deep work required for development. Externally, this has led to other schools and providers seeking training and coaching from the school and from Complete, who now have an education branch.

Recommended Reading

Campbell, J. and van Nieuwerburgh, C. (2018), *The Leader's Guide to Coaching in Schools: Creating Conditions for Effective Learning.* UK: Corwin.

Carter, D. and McInerney, L. (2021), *Leading Academy Trusts: Why Some Fail, but Most Don't.* UK: John Catt Publishing.

Harcombe, K. (2010), *How to Survive and Succeed as a Headteacher.* UK: LDA.

Rees, T. (2017), *Wholesome Leadership.* UK: John Catt Publishing.

Snape, R. (2021), *The Headteacher's Handbook: The Essential Guide to Leading a Primary School.* UK: Bloomsbury Education.

References

Adair, J. (2009), *Effective Communication (Revised Edition): The Most Important Management Skill of All* (Most Important Management Tool of All). UK: Pan.

Association or School and College Leader's (ASCL) (2020), *Framework for Ethical Leadership in Education.* UK: ASCL. Available at: ASCL - Framework for ethical leadership in education (Accessed: 01.09.2021).

Beabout, R. (2012), 'Turbulence, Perturbance, and Educational Change'. *Complicity: An International Journal of Complexity and Education*, 9(2), pp. 15–29, Available at: (3) Beabout Feature Article (ed.gov) (Accessed: 01.09.2021).

Berry, J. (2016), *Making the Leap: Moving from Deputy to Head*. UK: Crown House Publishing.

Bird, J. and Gornall, S. (2016), *The Art of Coaching: A Handbook of Tips and Tools*. Oxon: Routledge.

Buck, A. (2016), *Leadership Matters*, UK: John Catt Publication.

Cameron, E. and Green, M. (2019), *Making Sense of Change Management: A Complete Guide to the Models, Tools, and Techniques of Organisational Change*, 5th edn. London: Kogan Page.

DfE (2020), *Headteachers' Standards 2020*. UK: DfE. Available at: Headteachers' standards 2020 - GOV.UK (www.gov.uk) (Accessed: 01.09.2021).

Fullan, M. (2020), *Nuance: Why Some Leaders Succeed, and Others Fail*. UK: Corwin.

Hill, M. (2002), *School Leadership and Complex Theory*. UK: Routledge.

Pain, M. (2019), *Being the CEO: Six Dimensions of Educational Leadership*. UK: John Catt.

Skinner, J. and Oberholzer, L. (2020), *Learning Conversations with Future Leaders. A Practice Insight Working Paper*. UK: CollectiveED. Available at: CollectivED Working Papers (leedsbeckett.ac.uk) (Accessed: 01.09.2021).

Sinek, S. (2011), *Start with Why: How Great Leaders Inspire Everyone to Take Action*. UK: Penguin.

Weick, K. (1995), *Sensemaking in Organisations*. London: Sage.

8

Mentoring and Coaching Women in Leadership

Lizana Oberholzer and Vivienne Porritt

Aims and Objectives

- To explore why coaching and mentoring play a vital role in supporting aspirational, future, and existing female leaders in education,
- To explore how mentoring and coaching support can help women to progress to leadership roles in education,
- To explore what considerations are needed to be made when supporting women through mentoring and coaching in education.

Coaching and Mentoring Women into Leadership Introduction

Women play an important role in leading in education. The work of organisations such as WomenEd highlights the importance of grassroots organisations and how they support women through mentoring and coaching to enable them to progress to leadership.

Analysis of the School Workforce Census (2021) highlights that 74 per cent of primary headteachers are women as are 62 per cent of headteachers of Special Schools and Pupil Referral Units. In the secondary sector, 40 per cent of headteachers are women. Looked at in another way, 'In primary, men are present at senior level at a ratio of almost 2:1 of their representation at teaching level. A similar picture emerges in secondary; 34 per cent of classroom teachers are male but this increases to 60 per cent for headteachers' (School Workforce Census, 2021).

Women play a pivotal role as role models to inspire the future generation of female leaders in education, whether it is in schools or in Higher Education. According to Hewitt (2020) and Osho (2018), 56.6 per cent of the university student body comprise of women. The higher education workforce, however, reflects a different picture, where 45.3 per cent of the workforce are women, as outlined by the Higher Education Statistics Agency's (HESA) data. What is interesting to note is that the representation of women in the leadership and management workforce is even lower at 27.5 per cent. Osho (2018) highlights that apart from the challenges of low female representation in leadership in higher education, there are also concerns regarding British Minority Ethnic (BME) female representation and that 0.5 per cent of UK female professors are Black. To ensure that women continue to inspire the next generation of future leaders, and break through the glass ceiling of attaining top leadership roles, mentoring and coaching can play an important part in enabling colleagues.

The statistics emphasize the importance of continuing to support female colleagues to progress and develop into specific leadership roles. Mentoring and coaching, as cognitive leadership skills, can play an important role in helping women to develop their confidence and unlock their own potential to take the next step into leadership roles. Targeted mentoring and coaching to support women is key; however, developing mentoring and coaching approaches within organisations, to help unlock the potential of future leaders, will also help to break through the barriers women face when aiming to progress to leadership roles.

Porritt and Featherstone (2019) address at length the importance of tackling these imbalances to help develop aspirational and future leaders at all levels. This is an important opportunity to ensure that the workforce becomes more representative in relation to the leadership roles women hold and how they can contribute to the education landscape in future.

Sandberg (2015) reflects on the fact that she had hoped that the situation had changed for women in society since her university days; however, the sad reality is that women are often faced with a wide range of challenges. Sandberg (2015) makes the point that women often need to balance all the societal demands plus a very challenging career, and she refers to the fact that they balance two careers, that of a full-time wife and parent as well as their professional career, which can often make it even more difficult to progress compared to their male counterparts.

During Covid-19, Sandberg's views regarding women's roles as carers once again came under the spotlight. The Chartered Institute of Personnel and Development (CIPD) outlined in a recent report led by the University of Sheffield that there are 3.7 million working carers in England and Wales and that a number of individuals had to balance dual roles. According to the report published by the Chartered Institute for Personnel and Development (CIPD) (2020), 'women are more likely than men to find it difficult to combine their job and caring responsibilities'. In addition, the report also stated:

One in five working carers had taken paid leave to fulfil their caring responsibilities. There was a gender difference in taking paid leave: 25% of men had been able to take paid leave to provide care, compared with 15% of women.

What was interesting regarding the report was that 'men find it easier than women to take an hour or two during work to attend to family or personal matters'.

According to UK Aid (2020), women outnumber men in the informal work industries too. Women often need to make allowances for caring for their families alongside a very busy career, which often means that women's progression in the workplace is slower, or they consider different avenues and pathways to move forward. As the pandemic highlighted, women often take a step back when there are life challenges, and they are often also experiencing different challenges regarding benefits as illustrated in the above regarding paid leave. Sandberg (2015) also points out that women often plan how their life journeys will unfold, consider how their families might grow and often put themselves forward for promotions or next steps while still aiming to be considerate of their employers. However, Sandberg (2015) stresses that it might take longer than nine months before a woman needs to be away from work on maternity leave and that women must start to think in a more progressive way about their careers.

In addition, Sandberg (2015) states that, despite the day-to-day challenges, women are also acutely aware of the Heidi and Howard effect. The Heidi and Howard effect outlines that women are often viewed in a negative light if they convey similar traits in the workplace to their male counterparts, and they are often disliked for these if they are in leadership roles. However, men are perceived in a positive light when they convey these traits. Women are, therefore, subconsciously aware of how they might impact on others, how they are perceived and of coming across as ambitious or keen to progress on their journeys, so often they need to draw on more subtle ways to develop into leadership roles and gain the support of peers.

Women often report a lack of confidence in applying for roles and often feel that they are not equipped or qualified enough for their next role. Cowley (2019) in Porritt and Featherstone (2019) cites the Drawing Future report by Cambers et al. (2018), which points out that girls often select caring roles, whereas boys often select more practical roles when they need to consider careers, and she makes the valid point that we need to challenge the systemic issues that help shape these perceptions at such an early age.

Peacock (2019), as cited in Porritt and Featherstone (2019), states that 'it takes guts to push for change, but the reality is that when we begin to work together, everything gets easier and seems possible'. It is therefore important to reflect on how a collaborative professional approach (Hargreaves and O'Connor, 2018), such as mentoring and coaching, will enable women to progress and move forward on their learning journeys as future and aspirational leaders.

What Mentoring and Coaching Is Not When Supporting Future Women into Leadership

When looking at coaching and mentoring practices, it is fair to say that they vary greatly and that there are many ways in which learning conversations are framed or conducted to support others. However, this chapter does not aim to advocate any specific approach, and it does not advocate practices which perhaps are put in place as 'quick fixes' to pay lip service to supporting women to progress on their leadership journey. This chapter aims to consider how learning conversations can be shaped through mentoring and coaching to offer support for women's development.

This chapter draws on, as earlier explored in Chapter 1, Connor and Pokora's (2016) definition of mentoring and coaching as a learning relationship. We want to emphasize the importance of relationships, and the importance of developing trusting relationships, to help support women's needs on their various career journeys. In this chapter the focus is not on practices, such as speed coaching, or ten-minute coaching sessions. The aim is to focus on how to support women in a sustained way, where coaching and mentoring become part of their professional self-care toolkit and part of their own professional development, and growth journey.

Speed coaching, similar to speed dating, is an interesting concept; however, based on the core definitions of coaching and mentoring, as explored in the Introduction and earlier chapters of this book, the authors state that mentoring and coaching are founded in trusting relationships with a skilled coach or mentor with the aim to meet the needs of the coachee. Speed coaching, as a concept, can only provide a taster of a potential learning conversation. And, at best, it offers a very narrow take on how the coaching conversation needs to be conducted and how it provides the coachee with the learning opportunities required to support them to move forward. Often these speed coaching events happen as a one-off event and are without future engagements or follow-ups to ensure that the coachee can continue to develop. There are, of course, benefits to offering support, and many colleagues will feel that it was helpful as an initial starting point to stimulate their thinking to engage with speed coaching. However, there is also the risk that such initiatives can only scratch the surface, and the coachee and mentee might not fully reap the benefits of fully developed coaching and mentoring practices, which leaves them feeling unsupported over time. For the purpose of this chapter, the authors are only exploring coaching and mentoring practices which aim to engage with a sustained, trusting coaching relationship, where the needs of the mentee or coachee is carefully considered in line with the EMCC's (2021) and ICF's (2021) ethical guidance. Hardingham, as cited in Passmore (2021), states that understanding the needs of the coachee is imperative, and that can only happen in a structured, sustained coaching relationship.

Sharing Stories and Narrative Coaching

Most women often experience significant challenges on their various career journeys, whether it is due to family commitments, care duties or bias in the workplace; most women often find it difficult to progress, and to get the appropriate support. WomenEd exemplifies this in conversations through social media. One tweet describes lost hopes and waste:

> I think for me it would be to be asked early on in your career what your plan is (perhaps during [your] NQT year) and having a mentor to help you put steps into place. I wanted to be a leader since my NQT year and had to make it up or work out what to do, implement and pay for it myself (Slater, 2019).

WomenEd, as a grassroots organisation, provides excellent opportunities for women to share their experiences and situations with a wide range of experienced leaders and coaches. Sandberg and Tsoukas (2015) highlight the importance of sense making, and through narrative coaching and mentoring practices, women in education are able to share their experiences with their communities of practice, in a safe space, with the aim to find solutions for these challenges. The power of coaching and mentoring can inspire hope and success.

Most women often doubt themselves; for example, Yamina Bibi shares how her inner critic impacted on her as she states, '[it] told me I had to be perfect all the time and [it] regularly told me that I was not good enough!' (Bibi, 2021). Bukky Yusuf, Yamina's coach from the WomenEd community, helped her 'to think differently'. Yamina shares that her coach helped her 'to become more aware of [herself]' and to 'find [her] inner strength beyond anything [she] knew even existed within [her]'. Yamina went on to be a network leader in WomenEd and a senior leader in several schools.

Bentley (2020) points out that if coachees are not enabled to share their experiences and practices, they often, especially if they experience particular challenges, revert back to their negative narratives instead of looking to the future during their coaching conversations. To ensure that women in education are heard and truly valued, there is a key need for them to share their experiences in a collaborative professional space and then move into an opportunity to think about solutions when they are ready to do so. Narrative coaching practices provide safe spaces for this to happen. This is also why the authors advocate against very short-term solutions regarding coaching. Hollweck and Lofthouse (2021) outline the importance of contextual coaching and how it is important for coaches to understand the needs of the coachee in full to ensure that their needs are met.

Narrative Coaching Models

Drake's (2017) narrative coaching model is a useful model to use to help shape these conversations, as it acknowledges the events that led up to where most women are, but it also highlights how key points can be reconsidered and reframed with the future in mind. Below is an adaptation of the model which can be used in conversations with women to reflect on their experiences, the here and now and how to move the focus towards the future with a positive mindset.

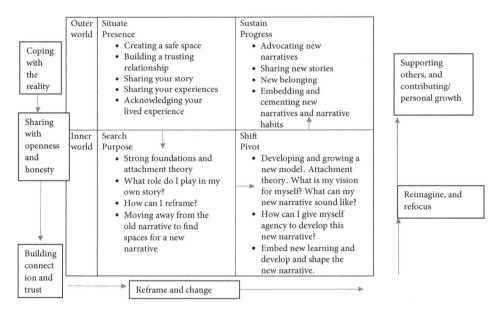

Figure 8.1 Drake's (2017) narrative coaching model.

Drake's (2017) model is a helpful framework to use. It is often used over four coaching sessions where each part of the framework is explored. The framework outlines the importance of creating a calm, safe space to allow the mentee or coachee to come to terms with what has happened and to enable them to cope with the situation first. Once this phase is addressed, and a relationship of trust, as well as a strong rapport between the coach and the coachee, is in place, the coach can progress and move forward to support the coachee on the journey. The key is that the coachee feels safe and has a willingness to progress and move forward, with the aim to create a new narrative. Drake (2017) points out that it is key that the coachee is enabled and experiences a non-judgemental engagement with the coach, so the coachee is able to steer her own learning journey. The coach needs to adhere to the six narrative coaching principles:

- The coach and coachee need to trust that the solutions are within the coachee. This commitment to 'unlock' the individual's potential, as discussed in Chapter 1, is a key coaching principle, as outlined by Whitmore (2017). However, at times, as Buck (2020) points out, there is a place for supporting and providing guidance with permission, and it is important to know when to mentor and when to coach, and this will be discussed further below.
- Both coach and coachee need to be fully present, and in the moment during the coaching session. It is imperative that the coachee drives the journey and that the coach does not draw on her own narratives and stories. Of course, there are moments where we need to emphasize, but empathy does not mean we share all our narratives. We need to put ourselves in the shoes of our coachees to ensure that they can trust us to help them to unpack their stories and to feel valued (Covey, 2010). Phrases such as 'I can see that it is very difficult for you', 'similar experiences are shared by other women', 'can you tell me more about it?' are often very useful to draw on to ensure that those experiencing challenges are helped to open up and reflect more openly. Bentley (2020) describes coaching as 'light and nimble'. When you get into the detail of your own experiences, and that of others, it often becomes more difficult to progress and move forward. Thomson (2013) advocates that 'what' and 'how' questions are often the most helpful at this stage, as they enable deep reflection and encourage the coachee to consider where they are at and how they can move forward. 'Why' questions can often have a more challenging impact, as they can lead to defensiveness, and the coachee might revert to a limbic response, which can lead to a fight, flight or freeze reaction. Holding the conversation in the moment in a calm state will enable the coachee to progress to the next stage where solutions are explored creatively to change the narrative.
- Kline (2020) advocates that it is important not to interrupt the flow of the coachee, and she stresses the importance to hold the silence to enable the coachee to develop their narrative and thinking fully. It is important to ensure that the narrative can flow; however, there is a careful balance between the moments of silence and the use of active listening techniques such as paraphrasing, playback and summaries (Buck, 2020; Bentley, 2020). The coach will need to make key judgements throughout the conversation to know when would be the most

appropriate moment to play information back and when to not interrupt to help the coachee to unpack their thinking carefully.

- Drake (2017) points out that the focus needs to be on general experiences and not long explanations, which aligns with Bentley's view (2020) that coaching needs to be 'light and nimble'. In order for the coachee to progress to the next stage, they need to acknowledge what happened, but it is also important to them look ahead at the next stage and steps.
- It is important to work with the narratives provided and to draw on the coachee's language and shared experiences to ensure that they can reflect on the here and now and on how to move forward. Drawing on the metaphors used is an important technique to enable the coachee to unpack their narratives clearly (Thomson, 2013).
- As a new narrative is emerging and growing from the coaching, the coach needs to stand on the 'threshold' of this narrative and allow the coachee to shape her own narrative, in a non-judgemental way. So often coaches feel that they need to add their view or flavour to the narrative at this stage. However, it is important to enable the coachee to shape their new journey in an authentic way, to help them to articulate the new narrative and to develop new habits to share the narrative and for it to become part of their journey.

When to Coach and When to Mentor

In Chapter 1, it was discussed how mentors and coaches need to know when to mentor, when to be nurturing, and when to coach. The same principles apply to coaching women in education and particularly when we look at narrative coaching. At times, when someone is new to sharing stories, or the teaching profession, more nurturing approaches and direction are needed until a strong trusting relationship is in place and the colleague is able to progress to the next level of their coaching journey, where asking more questions becomes more appropriate and enables them to challenge their own thinking. It is key for the coach to understand how to move on the continuum of coaching and mentoring within the coaching relationship (Buck, 2020). Asking challenging questions too early in the coaching journey might have a negative impact on the colleague, as they might feel too fragile to be challenged at that stage. However, once they can share their narrative, and understand that it is a lived experience that is important to acknowledge and which forms part of the body of lived experiences for many women in education, they will progress. As illustrated in Clutterbuck and Lane's (2004) model, they become more independent, and ready to be coached through open questioning. Progressing through the continuum of coaching and mentoring is a key skill to ensure that colleagues are fully supported and their individual needs are met. The authors also advocate that it is important that mentors and coaches have an in-depth understanding of when to coach and when to mentor to ensure that they offer appropriate support to those they support.

Mentoring Women into Leadership – Exploring the Challenges Women Often Face

Women face a variety of challenges in both their personal and professional lives. We explored some of these in the introduction. When making the leap into leadership, women often feel that leadership roles are designed for men by men. Before applying for a leadership role, women need to be more than 10 per cent braver, as the WomenEd mantra suggests, as they often feel that they don't meet all the requirements for the role. Porritt (2018) highlights that language in job advertisements may put women off in applying for senior leadership roles. In *The Guardian*, Porritt (2018) states that:

> words such as 'driven' and 'ambitious' – especially when repeated within a three or four-paragraph job advert – are a turn-off for women seeking to apply for senior roles. 'It's just not how they see themselves or how they want to do leadership when they get there'. In addition, women often experience challenges at interviews, such as being the only woman in the room or being interviewed by an all-male panel. Often the language and practices of an organisation favour men in relation to promotions, as outlined by Sandberg (2015). Practices during the pandemic demonstrated how women are often drawing on the 'shortest straw' when it comes to work opportunities, benefits and family commitments.

Women therefore have more challenging narratives to share, and by the time they get to the point where they seek help, and ask to be mentored or coached, they are often in a position where they are traumatized by their experiences. It is often best, when a colleague in this scenario seeks help to provide them with nurturing support and mentor them to a calmer space, where they are able to start reflecting in a more challenging way on next steps and ways forward. Being mindful of the needs of the individual here is key, and moving on the continuum of coaching and mentoring will make all the difference to help empower colleagues to grow and flourish in a nurturing way.

Mentoring Women into Leadership – Exploring How to Empower Women to Move Forward with Their Career Goals and Focus

This chapter outlines how narrative coaching can be used to help women to (a) share their stories, and (b) reconstruct their narratives, with the aim to foster new narrative habits. The key is to enable women to use their own language to acknowledge that they are valuable contributors to the wider education context. They need to engage with their own career journey without apologising for what they can contribute and without feeling that the Heidi and Howard effect can impact negatively on their journey (Sandberg, 2015). In addition, women need to stand proud, advocate their work and share their achievements with others, thus being powerful role models for other women to look up to and enable them to achieve.

As mentors who nurture future leaders, we need to help enable women to change the narrative and discourse. We need to nurture them not to apologize for who they are and what they achieve (Featherstone, 2019). As mentors, we need to encourage language that acknowledges the achievements of each individual.

Women, however, often draw on pronouns such as 'we' when talking about their own achievements. They also need to acknowledge their role with pride and start using personal pronouns (Part et al., 2021) to reflect their contributions to the success of their organisations more clearly. When playing back conversations, and discussing achievements, phrases such as 'how did you contribute' and 'how did you help the team succeed' are useful questions to ask to encourage female leaders to start acknowledging their contributions more consistently and help them articulate their success. 'What are your next steps?' and 'what are your future goals' are useful questions to ask to normalize conversations regarding female ambition and to normalize women having a career plan. Authors such as Sandberg (2015) highlight how women often think about their next step in their career only after they think about family planning. However, she makes the point that it is often still nine months before any changes might need to be considered, and there is nothing wrong with considering a promotion or next steps. Mentoring women around these issues means that mentors also need to be 10 per cent braver in their conversations to challenge the thinking that often places a glass ceiling on women's considerations for their next steps.

Mentoring and Coaching Women to Drive Their Goals

If mentoring women into acknowledging their own work is key, helping women to set goals for themselves and to map their career pathway will help them to normalize the discussions around wanting to have a career and succeeding beyond their family life commitments. So often, women will say that they did not feel that they could move forward on their journey due to their other commitments. Sandberg (2015) makes the points that women need to have more open conversations with their other halves about engaging with family life in partnership rather than just one member of the family doing the lion's share of the work. As mentors, conversations such as these can be developed and rehearsed to enable women to help articulate these thoughts and map out how these conversations can be shaped. Similarly, in the workplace, women often report that they are given roles that are less challenging and accept the stereotype that they won't be interested in roles such as curriculum design, timetabling and data analysis. In fact, women are often very good at organisational work, mapping and working with numbers. It is a key role for mentors to play significant role in helping colleagues to practise and shape conversations to challenge these stereotypes and to learn how to negotiate what roles they would like to undertake. Women often do not negotiate, and it is a core skill to help women to develop on their leadership journey.

Mentoring and Coaching Women from Cradle to Headship

The authors acknowledge that mentoring and coaching practices need to be in place for school leaders at all levels to support them on their leadership journey. However, we want to stress that giving women in education agency to lead must start from the outset of their journey. Supporting women in education from their initial teacher journey through to leadership is vital to address the gender balance narrative and to enable women to have agency as future leaders. Porritt and Oberholzer (2019) highlight the importance of initial teacher trainees engaging with mentoring and coaching as well as engaging with the WomenEd community. This develops their ability to apply for future roles and to negotiate their roles and salaries more constructively, so women in education find themselves in stronger position regarding their roles, conditions and salaries.

Supporting Initial Teacher Trainees (ITT) to complete their application documents and to write their applications in a less descriptive and more focused way will make all the difference.

From experience, the authors know that women often don't tend to apply for roles if they don't meet all the criteria outlined in the job description. Porritt (2021) highlighted that men often apply for roles if they only meet 60 per cent of the criteria. When mentoring women, the important issue is to enable them to realize that they can and should apply for interesting roles and that they have potential to grow into the roles as their male counterparts do. In addition, they need to look at their current experience, and produce application forms and statements that align with the job description and requirements. They need to demonstrate how they are a strategic and best fit candidate for the role, rather than just listing all their achievements. In addition, they need to develop the confidence to demonstrate that their achievements can be transferred to their new context and improve key issues within the organisation.

As part of the mentoring process, mentors work through model application forms highlighting positive language use and approaches to enable them to move forward. Once the application is submitted, and the interview is secured, the mentor and mentee can move forward to the next phase of the preparations, where the applicant can then work through a series of potential questions. The key is to think how the candidate needs to arrive, how the first handshake makes an impression and what impression they want to make. Often conversations are also around what to wear. However, the biggest focus during the mentoring conversations should be around how to apply and how to address the interview questions.

The most important point is that the mentee needs to avoid apologetic language if they are highlighting their work and achievements. They need to learn how to use 'I' rather than 'we', and stress how they enabled others, or what they did to achieve certain things. When responding to questions, they also need to evidence success and their impact. They need to highlight how they will tackle the issue, what they did in the past, how it made a difference and how they can draw on these experiences to improve outcomes in their new context (Porritt, 2021). It is an invaluable opportunity for colleagues to ensure that they are prepared for interviews. Through this nurturing process, mentors can be helpful sounding boards to enable the colleague they are supporting to really think carefully how she shapes her response and prepares for the role.

Furthermore, end of interview responses can also be considered. Are they still interested in the role? What might the salary, timetable and working pattern look like? What other requirements might there be in terms of travel or moving, for example? How should this be considered?

Women often do not address these issues at all or very late in the conversation regarding their work conditions, and often at that point it is very challenging to change anything. These practices need to be developed from the start of the teacher's journey, rather than addressed later on when they realize that their work-life challenges are impossible to manage.

Mentoring and Coaching Women to Embrace the New Role with Confidence

However, it is often one thing to land the role and another to move into the role and engage with it with confidence. Women often struggle with imposter syndrome when they start a new role. Mentoring and coaching provide an invaluable support platform for women to help sound out challenges safely, and it enables them to explore solutions to an array of issues without feeling that they are being judged. Having safe spaces, with like-minded people, can have a profound impact on how women can move forward on their journey. Mentoring and coaching need to become normalized and part of women's self-care toolkit, as it should be for all school leaders, to help them to navigate the start of their leadership journey all the way to headship.

Leaders often need a safe space where they can make sense of their challenges before they can give sense to others (Sandberg and Tsoukas, 2015). Schools often use coaching and mentoring as ways to address underperformance; however, we argue that coaching and mentoring should be embedded in support practice for leaders to unlock their potential and help them to think through challenges, rather than make split second decisions without evaluating the impact. Too much is at stake.

As explained in Chapter 1, mentoring can be hugely helpful to a novice teacher or leader in navigating an unfamiliar landscape. As they become more confident, the mentor can move on the continuum of coaching and mentoring to provide thinking spaces and challenge to help the leader evaluate their strategic decisions more carefully before sharing with their teams and to support their teams more effectively. Being challenged in a safe space through open questions helps leaders to also anticipate the future questions they might face and how they can mitigate the challenges that their teams might present. This is a healthy way to give leaders confidence in their ability to make key decisions and to think strategically. More opportunities to support new leaders need to be in place to help leaders grow in their confidence and to make a flying start on their journey.

Being faced with ethical dilemmas is often one of the most common challenges new leaders can encounter, and Stearns' ethicability model is a useful conversation tool that a coach can use with a new school leader to help them think it through:

Steare's (2006) 'ethicability' approach:

- Are we acting with integrity?
- Who is this good for?

- Who could we harm?
- What's the truth? Are we willing to be open, honest and accountable for our actions?

During the coaching conversation, the coach simply asks the above questions to enable the coachee to talk through the dilemma they are facing. During the conversation, the coach draws on active listening strategies, such as playing back, checking in and getting summaries, for example:

- 'what I am hearing is …',
- ' you are using x … tell me more about that',
- 'you are sharing an issue that is really worrying you, tell me more …'.

Once all the questions are explored, the coach will aim to ask the coachee:

'In summary, after working through these questions, what do you feel your next step needs to be …?'

By asking the coachee to consolidate their strategic thinking, and explore ways forward by identifying next steps, they start thinking ahead more strategically, and creatively, and open up their thinking without limitations in mind. Often with ethical dilemmas, school leaders find it incredibly difficult to approach their team to discuss it, and Steare's model helps to think these issues through in a safe space, and to make a clear and considered decision on ways forward. The role of mentoring and coaching for women in education is twofold: first, it offers valuable support, guidance as well as nurturing opportunities, and second, it provides opportunities to help leaders to facilitate their thinking and to help them to grow into their future leadership roles.

Valuable Lessons and Experience Shared by Experienced Mentors and Coaches

Case Study

WomenEd London worked closely with the University of East London to lead on the very first Early Careers Teacher Unconference, the purpose of which was to provide future teachers with the opportunity to engage with WomenEd from the early stages of their careers. The aim was for women to engage in the conversation and change the narrative regarding inequalities for women in education by engaging with the employment process, and how they can prepare for their interviews as well as negotiate their outcomes. WomeEd London hosted a summer event where experienced practitioners shared their practice, stories and journeys with new teachers. The offer also included coaching and mentoring with Initial Teacher Trainees (ITT), providing an opportunity to engage with a mentor to gain advice on applying for roles and for support. Often ITTs reported that they did not feel worthy to apply for a teaching role and often applied for a Teaching Assistant (TA) role instead. The mentoring and coaching aimed to address this self-efficacy issue.

The learning from this engagement was that mentoring and coaching enabled new teachers in the profession to:

- talk to role models,
- feel supported and be guided in their practice,
- feel more empowered, and
- develop a sense of agency to apply for teaching roles.

Of the ITTs who engaged with the mentoring and coaching, 89 per cent of them gained a job as a Newly Qualified Teacher (NQT) for the following year. Where NQTs did not engage with mentoring or coaching support, 33 per cent of the cohort considered TA roles or moved on to do supply teaching instead. This case study reflects the importance of supporting future teachers, and in particular women, to enable them to develop confidence and the necessary skills to navigate recruitment processes effectively.

Reflective Task

Reflect on your own leadership story and write a 200-word journal reflection exploring your own narrative. When looking back:

- What was your main learning?
- What questions can you ask yourself with the future in mind?
- How can your story help others to succeed?
- What are your own next steps?
- How does capturing a story and reflecting on your journey help you to develop your reflective skills?

How can this technique be used to support other women in future?

Recommended Reading

Criado Perez, C. (2019), *Invisible Women: Exposing Data Bias in a World Designed for Men*. UK: Chatto and Windus.

Featherstone, K. and Porritt, V. (2020), *Being 10% Braver*. London: Sage.

Francke, A. (2019), *Create A Gender-Balance Workplace*. UK: Penguin.

Rippon, G. (2019), *The Gendered Brain: The New Neuroscience that Shatters the Myth of the Female Brain*. UK: Penguin Random House.

References

Austin, A. and Heyes, J. (2020), Supporting working carers: How employers and employees can benefit, research report, CIPD/University of Sheffield.

Bentley, R. (2020), Break-through conversations, Q595. Available at: https://q595-breakthrough-conversations.com/ (Accessed: 01. 09.2021).

Bibi, Y. (2021), *WomenEd Connecting Hearts and Minds*, WordPress, 21 September [Online]. Available at: https://msybeebs.wordpress.com/2021/09/25/womened-connecting-hearts-and-minds-across-london/ (accessed 17. 1.2022) https://msybeebs.wordpress.com/2021/09/25/womened-connecting-hearts-and-minds-across-london/.

CIPD (2020), 'Supporting working carers'. Available at: https://www.cipd.co.uk/Images/supporting-working-carers-2_tcm18-80339.pdf (Accessed: 01. 09.2021).

Drake, D. B. (2017), *Narrative Coaching: The Definitive Guide to Bringing New Stories to Life*. UK: CNC Press.

Durrant, J. (2019), *Teacher Agency, Professional Development and School Improvement*. Oxon: Routledge.

Hargreaves, E. and Rolls, L. (2021), *Unlocking Research: Reimagining Professional Development in Schools*. Oxon: Routledge.

Hollweck, T. and Lofthouse, R. M. (2021), 'Contextual coaching: levering and leading school improvement through collaborative professionalism', *International Journal of Mentoring and Coaching in Education*, https://doi.org/10.1108/IJMCE-01-2021-0019 (Accessed: 01. 09.2021).

Kline, N. (2020), *The Promise that Changes Everything: I Won't Interrupt You*, UK: Penguin.

Oberholzer, L. (2021), *Is There a Glass Ceiling in Higher Education?* UK: Sage. Available at: https://perspectivesblog.sagepub.com/blog/books/is-there-a-glass-ceiling-in-higher-education (Accessed: 01.09.2021).

Part, R., Page-Tickell, R., and Oberholzer, L. (2021), *Storytelling and Dialogue Providing Insight into Gendering and Its Intersection with Professional Identity in Post Experience Education*. UK: BAM.

Passmore, J. (2021), *The Coaches' Handbook: The Complete Practitioner Guide for Professional Coaches*. UK: Routledge.

Peacock, A. (2019) in Porritt, V. and Featherstone, K. (eds), *10% Braver: Inspiring Women to Lead Education*. London: Sage.

Porritt, V. and Featherstone, K. (eds) (2019), *10% Braver: Inspiring Women to Lead Education*. London: Sage Publishing.

Porritt, V. and Oberholzer, L. (2019). 'NQT Mentoring Can Improve Confidence and Retention'. *School Leadership Today* 10(1), pp. 42–5.

Porritt, V. (2021), 'Write a job application that gets results', *YouTube*, May, [Online]. Available at https://www.youtube.com/watch?v=H6iE_Ay6fao&t=1825s (accessed 17 January 2022).

Sandberg, J. and Tsoukas, H. (2015). 'Making sense of the sensemaking perspective: Its constituents, limitations, and opportunities for further development'. *Journal of Organizational Behaviour*, 36(S1), pp. S6–S32.

Slater, K. [@southwestsenco] (2019), 4 December [Twitter] Available at: https://twitter.com/southwestsenco/status/1202112412964605952?s=20 (accessed 17 January 2022).

Steare, R. (2006), *Ethicability*. UK: Dawne Books.

Tickle, L. (2018), 'Language in school job ads puts women off headteacher roles', *The Guardian*, 19 June [Online].Available at: https://www.theguardian.com/education/2018/jun/19/language-school-headteacher-job-ads-puts-women-off (accessed: 17 January 2022).

UK Aid (2020), Implications of COVID-19 on women informal workers (Accessed: 01. 09.2021) Available at: https://assets.publishing.service.gov.uk/government/uploads/system/uploads/attachment_data/file/911533/Query-53-covid-and-women-informal-workers.pdf.

9

Mentoring and Coaching BAME Colleagues in Education and into Leadership

Lizana Oberholzer and Amjad Ali

Aims and Objectives

- To develop a clear understanding of how to draw on coaching and mentoring skills to support leaders from Black, Asian and minority ethnic (BAME) groups into leadership roles,
- To develop a clear understanding of how and when to mentor and when to coach when supporting BAME colleagues into leadership roles.

Introduction

Garvey and Stokes (2022, p. 70) state 'that mentoring [and coaching are] based on valuing and working with individual differences and is predicated on beliefs about individual and collective agency, and collaborative potential to effect meaningful change'. Supporting BAME colleagues to develop and flourish as future leaders through the use of coaching and mentoring is a powerful way not only to develop strong learning relationships (Connor and Pokora, 2016) but to strengthen working relationships within educational contexts, such as schools, colleges and universities.

As mentioned in the previous chapter, Coalter (2018) and Francke (2019), both leaders in their respective fields, advocate the importance of diverse teams, in both education and business. However, one of the key challenges and questions is, why are we not embracing it in the true sense of the word in many education contexts?

In Chapter 8, the authors discussed the underrepresentation of women in education. What is interesting when looking at education is the lack of representation across diversity groups seems to be even more concerning. As mentioned in the previous chapter, Osho (2018), as cited in Oberholzer (2021), highlights that:

> Apart from the challenges of low female representation in leadership in higher education, there are also concerns regarding BAME female representation, and that 0.5% of UK female professors are black, and it's clear that these issues need urgent attention.

Furthermore, according to data shared by the Department for Education (DfE, 2016), the lack of BAME leaders reflects as follows: 3.1 per cent of heads in schools are from BAME backgrounds compared to the pupil population of 31.4 per cent in primary and 27.9 per cent of secondary. It is clear that the dataset is not reflecting the diversity of the pupil demographic in schools, and one of the questions to ask is, why might this be the case? Why do regular updates on diversity and inclusion, and the representation of school leaders, not get fully published annually to provide schools, and school leaders, with a clearer understanding of what is required and needed in relation to recruitment practices? Porritt (2021) pointed out in her conference address to the International Professional Development Association (IPDA) that WomenEd, for example, does a vast amount of work in collecting data and reporting on the situation for women. However, the question is, why do school leaders not receive a full overview of the current situation to enable them to be more strategic in their recruitment and practices within schools? Garner (2015) makes the case that if there are not strong role models in communities, learners won't have school leaders to aspire to and that you 'cannot be what you cannot see' (Rabiger, 2019, as cited in Porritt and Featherstone, 2019).

Coaching and Mentoring Colleagues from Diverse Backgrounds

When working with colleagues from diverse backgrounds, it is important to remember, as a coach or mentor, to ensure that you make colleagues feel safe and supported during these professional learning conversations (Maslow, 1943, as cited in Cameron and Green, 2020). It is often the case that colleagues have been challenged in many ways on their career pathways, and they might have had a wide range of experiences, some very inspirational and others far more challenging than expected. It is therefore imperative to provide the necessary support for colleagues to meet their needs to help them move forward on their journey. Oberholzer (2019) points out that colleagues from diverse backgrounds often have signs of low self-efficacy. They might have wonderful credentials but often feel that they are not able to meet the requirements for their next role or next step. In addition, BAME colleagues often feel undervalued and challenged by their situations (Elonga Mboyo, 2019), and it is therefore important to carefully consider how they need to be nurtured and supported on their journeys.

When to Coach and When to Mentor

In Chapter 8, the authors discussed the importance of continuing to develop a detailed understanding of how to move on the continuum of coaching and mentoring (Buck, 2020) to ensure that the needs of the mentee or coachee are fully met. Similar principals apply when supporting BAME coachees, and a narrative approach to mentoring and coaching, as advocated by Drake (2017), forms an important part of how BAMEed's coaching and mentoring programme is shaped to support colleagues on their learning journey. Bentley (2020), in his work, focusing on breakthrough conversations, emphasizes the importance of developing a trusting relationship with the mentee or coachee to ensure that they can engage on their learning journey, in a calm, limbic state. Creating a safe space is key to ensure that colleagues are able to open up to learning. However, when working with colleagues who experienced trauma or challenge on their development journeys, it is often the case that they need to navigate their way through those past experiences first, acknowledge them of their lived experience before they are ready to progress in a more mentor or coaching framed conversations.

Understanding when to mentor and when to coach is key in strengthening the relationship of trust with BAME colleagues. It is important to realize that each approach has its merits: mentoring provides guidance and support, whereas coaching provide opportunities to facilitate thinking. Understanding when support is needed, or when thinking needs to be explored, is a vital part of the coach's role. Asking a series of questions can often provoke a negative response. Thomson (2013) points out that it is often best to focus on reflections around 'what' and 'how' questions before coaches progress to 'why' questions, which could potentially lead to a more defensive response. In addition, the key is to ensure that the BAME colleague is feeling safe and supported, empowered to share their story and able to start making sense of the here and now. Mentoring is often the important first step in the sense-making process where conversations can be opened up. However, if a colleague is more advanced in their career, processing and thinking, the mentor or coach might also want to explore what is best for the colleague, in relation to mentoring or coaching, by exploring what the colleague might find the most useful. However, in the event that a coaching conversation requires more support, with permission, the coach can make a decision to move on the continuum of coaching and mentoring (Buck, 2020) to find an appropriate thinking space for the BAME colleague to help facilitate their thinking. It is therefore important that BAME mentors and coaches have a very clear understanding of what mentoring and coaching are to ensure that they can make clear and confident decisions on how to support and meet the needs of their mentees and coachees. Using Drake's (2017) narrative coaching framework is one way to facilitate the lived experiences of BAME colleagues, similar to women leaders in education, as explored in Chapter 8, to enable colleagues to find ways forward in relation to their own development and next steps.

Mentoring BAME Colleagues into Leadership – Exploring the Challenges BAME Colleagues Often Face

Oberholzer (2019) shared how BAME leaders often struggle with their own confidence, and in the research piece, the author shares examples of BAME leaders' need to challenge situations where they are perceived differently because of their appearance, or accents, and of how they need to bounce back from these challenges and work past the negative bias that these painful experiences might cause. When such events do take place, mentors and coaches can provide helpful lifelines, where stories are shared, experiences are acknowledged and new solutions can be considered to move forward.

It is imperative for these lived experiences to be acknowledged and for them not to be swept under the carpet. It is key to address these issues in a reflective way, to explore the learning gained from the situation and to consider how this can be addressed and challenged as well. Small (2019) highlights the important work disruptors do in challenging the status quo and by being a force for good who see and lead the change needed. Through the exploration of narratives and lived experiences, BAME leaders will continue to develop agency and confidence to play their role in shaping the future education landscape. Mentoring and coaching can play a powerful part in helping to reimagine this narrative.

Mentoring BAME Colleagues into Leadership – Exploring How to Empower BAME Colleagues to Move Forward with Their Career Goals and Focus

As mentioned earlier in the chapter, BAME colleagues and future leaders face challenges regarding self-efficacy (Porritt and Featherstone, 2019). Colleagues are often faced with self-doubt and imposter syndrome as a result of their experiences and the feedback they receive, as exemplified in Oberholzer (2019) for example, colleagues who hold exceptional qualifications and receive feedback that they don't look the part, or sound right, or that the learning community might not warm to them as a teacher, colleague or leader. As coaches and mentors, it is not possible to provide the counselling support required if these events had a devastating impact on colleagues, due to years of challenge. It is important to remember that as mentor or coach, it is required by the EMCC's (2021) ethical guidance that a coach or mentor need to assess the needs of a mentee or coachee and make a decision on whether coaching or mentoring is suitable for them or not. If not, from an ethical perspective, the key is to discuss this with them and ensure that they are aware on how to find the suitable support to enable them to grow. If counselling is a more appropriate avenue to pursue, it might be that the BAME colleague will want to return to coaching and mentoring at a later stage.

However, if coaching and mentoring are the suitable strategies for the BAME colleague, the key is to reflect with the colleague on where they are at. BAMEed does not prescribe to a specific coaching model because mentors or coaches must understand the need of the coachee and draw on the relevant framework or support tools to enable colleagues to unpack their thinking. However, there are a few strategies that often help to navigate the journey well.

For many BAME leaders and future leaders, it is often key to narrate their journey, and using Drake's (2017) narrative coaching approach often works well to acknowledge challenges and core issues. Once the coachee is in a positive state of full self-awareness, and in a more balanced space, it is often useful to complete a SWOT analysis.

It often works well to complete this reflective task together, exploring the mentee or coachee's strengths. They are often surprised by what they can outline in this section. Moving on to the next section is often interesting, as the word 'weaknesses' often evokes a whole range of challenges, and it might be useful to refine the language use when you ask the question as a coach or mentor by phrasing it in a slightly more nuanced way: 'What areas do you still need to continue to refine?' Once explored you might want to progress to do some blue-sky thinking by exploring potential opportunities by asking, 'What opportunities are available to you that you can explore?' You might also want to provide the colleague with an opportunity to explore potential challenges by asking; 'What are the potential barriers?' Note how these questions are more nuanced than when using the word 'threats', which might trigger very negative and defensive responses. It often works best to frame the question more positively.

Once the SWOT analysis is complete, useful questions can be:

- What surprised you about the SWOT analysis?
- What are you learning about yourself and your journey?

- Based on this exercise, what possible targets do you feel you might want to work on?

At this stage, you can then move into one of the various coaching models such as the GROW model or the BASIC coaching method (Buck, 2020). It is a longer journey to get to a stage where colleagues are ready to be mentored or coached, but it is felt, based on BAMEed's experience over the past six years, that it is worth spending the time to develop trust, safety and clarity before BAME colleagues can comfortably move forward through a more solutions focused approach, without reverting back to the narratives and experiences they previously had. Doing a SWOT analysis is a simple framework to use; however, it draws on some of the principles outlined by Seligman's (2011) PERMA model, which advocates for promoting positive emotions, engagement and positive relationships, meaning and accomplishments. By celebrating these key aspects and enabling colleagues to see the positive and their contribution more frequently, it makes a huge impact on the development of their confidence, self-awareness and self-belief.

Mentoring and Coaching BAME Colleagues to Drive Their Goals

During the BAMEed coaching and mentoring development work that the charity did with school leaders, the key learning was that a large number of colleagues experienced the negative responses and feedback intensely, and it is key to be aware of the impact of negative bias. Grenville-Cleave (2016) highlights that negative feedback or responses are often experienced more strongly than positive ones, and it is key to understand what the impact of negative bias is. It is therefore important for BAME coaches or mentors to have a detailed understanding of how to frame and phrase questions more positively, and how it can help support BAME colleagues in reframing their own thinking regarding their future career journeys.

Enabling the coachee or mentee to see what is possible and how to move forward is a key part of the mentor or coach's role. It is imperative to help the coachee or mentee to see beyond the here and now and look to the future. That is why, using a framework such as a SWOT analysis is useful, as it helps the BAME colleague to reflect on what they can offer, what their strengths are and what their opportunities are, as well as helping them to acknowledge challenges with the mindset of addressing them in a positive way to enable the colleague to move forward.

By acknowledging challenges, and exploring possible solutions, it makes all the difference in developing a positive growth mindset in regard to future obstacles as well (Dweck, 2010). By reflecting on the coachee or mentee's narrative, and how the narrative can be reframed, it helps colleagues to see the potential opportunities that will drive their own personal goals regarding leadership development in a more positive way. Small (2019) highlights the importance of being a disrupter to lead necessary change. Through mentoring and coaching, the reframing of narratives can start in a safe space, where the emphasis can be shifted to what is possible as opposed to the negatives (Drake, 2017). It is important to recognize that this work does take time and that mentors or coaches need to commit to the journey with their mentees or coachees. Short, single coaching and mentoring sessions are often insufficient for this work, and relationships of trust are key to ensure that colleagues are fully supported (Buck, 2020).

Mentoring and Coaching BAME Colleagues to Apply for Leadership Roles

It is often useful, when working with aspirational leaders, to work in a targeted way on their career goals. They might often, as mentioned in the above, outline their challenges; however, there will be a point where colleagues will start to become more specific in their conversations with their mentors and coaches. Career progression is one of the key areas colleagues need support with.

Based on the BAMEed support offered over a number of years, it is interesting to do an initial analysis of what mentees or coachees applied for in the past, and it is often good to unpack and analyse how colleagues constructed the application. Based on the cases supported by BAMEed, mentors and coaches, it came to light that there are quite a large number of issues that can be addressed in leadership application forms which can make an immediate positive impact regarding potential recruitment processes and the candidate's ability to be short listed. The analysis revealed that candidates often list their achievements and accomplishments in their letters of application as well as their personal statements. These documents often don't address the job specifications specifically. Learning how to develop a more specific and strategic application, addressing the requirements of the job application and demonstrating how the candidate's skills are suitable and transferable to the role often make a huge difference in the chances of a candidate being short listed. It is quite commonplace for BAME colleagues to want to demonstrate their 'worth' and that they are the most qualified person for the role, and often they hold a wide range of outstanding qualifications. However, what will make a significant impact is for candidates to shape their applications more strategically in order to demonstrate what they can contribute, bring to the table, and, with their skills and qualifications in mind, how they can fulfil the role.

It is often useful for coaches and mentors to analyse the initial approaches to see whether the above might be an issue. A helpful technique, after analysing previous applications, is to ask the coachee or mentee to look at two or three job advertisements and identify what the key specifications for the roles are. This is a helpful first step, and often when coaches or mentors reflect on their working practice here, they need to move on the continuum of coaching and mentoring, as discussed in Chapters 1 and 8. Often a mentoring approach is more helpful to enable colleagues to collaborate on developing the coachee or mentee's skills and approaches to application forms and personal statements until they are able to shape their practices more independently. It often works well to work with the colleague on shaping their letter of application to address the full range of the specifications as well as their personal statement. Using the criteria as signposts in the letter and personal statement will make a big difference on how the piece is structured. In addition, supporting the mentee or coachee to reflect on specific examples from their practice to illustrate how they addressed certain points in similar contexts, what their impact was and how they would hope to contribute in a similar way in their new contexts will help shape the strategic element of the letter of application and personal statement. Working with the mentee or coachee in this way will help develop their understanding of how to approach their applications for leadership and senior roles more strategically to help them to demonstrate that they are well suited to the role. Once this aspect of the process is in hand, it is often important to start thinking about next steps, and potential interviews. Once again, depending on the stage the mentee or coachee is at, the coachee or mentor needs to decide how to move on the continuum of coaching and mentoring to suitably support the colleague they are working with.

Mentoring and Coaching BAME Colleagues to Prepare for the Interview Process

Self-efficacy is a key factor, which can impact on the outcome of recruitment processes for BAME colleagues, as explored earlier in the chapter. It is therefore important to help colleagues prepare for their interviews. It is often the case that a mentoring approach is more suitable in the initial stages of preparation. BAMEed mentors draw on a bank of questions for interview preparation which are suitable for each leadership phase to prepare candidates for their interviews. In the initial preparation, colleagues work through questions and ask candidates to reflect on their possible answers by considering the job requirements carefully. Techniques such as repeating or paraphrasing the question are practised during the mentoring session to allow thinking time. For example, once a question on how the mentee would tackle a challenge in their new role is paraphrased, the mentor will work with the mentee to develop a response in which they outline how they will address the issue, provide an example of how they did address it in the past, what the impact was and how they are hoping to refine their practice for their new employer going forward. Once the mentor worked through three to four questions with the mentee, they are asked to then plan responses for an additional six questions, which they will share with their mentor via email to feedback on. Once the mentee feels more confident in approaching the questions, the mentor arranges a mock interview opportunity.

Similar preparations are provided for the colleague to reflect on their body language, non-verbal cues and how they want to ensure that they come across in the best possible way at interview. Kostic and Chadee (2015) highlight the importance of being aware of non-verbal communication and how it can have a profound effect on the outcome of interviews. It is therefore important to reflect with the mentee on how they can convey their skills and what they can offer in the best possible way.

Prior to the interview, mentors also work with mentees on the importance of researching the context well, and they work through the school's website, policies and ethos in full; key conversations are engaged with as well, to ensure that the context is suitable for the mentee. It is important to find a context where you can be the best you can be, and it is important to ensure that your values align fully with the organisation that you are working with. Misalignment can have a challenging impact on the future leader's engagement with their new organisation, and it is important that the applicant considers that aspect of their journey carefully too. It is, of course, exciting to be invited for interview, and a new role that naturally the applicant is working towards, but it is important to find the right organization for you to flourish in too.

Mentoring and Coaching BAME Colleagues to Embrace the New Role with Confidence

It is important to realize that, once the leader landed the role, they will need further support. In the earlier chapters of the book, it was discussed how the Dreyfus Model (Dreyfus and Dreyfus, 1986) needs to be considered when developing into a new role, for example, as a teacher or when colleagues develop into a role as a leader.

New roles often mean that you start as a novice. Your level of experience of previous roles might mean that your development trajectory is quicker and that you might move on to proficient levels or expert levels at an accelerated pace. However, it is still important to have the necessary support in place to start the journey with confidence. Cameron and Green (2020) highlight the importance of coaching and mentoring as cognitive skills that can help others to develop. As part of a leader's, and in particular a new leader's, self-care toolkit, it is essential to have a mentor or coach to support them on their journey. Mentoring and coaching provide a safe learning space to enable new leaders to make sense of their new learning journey in their new leadership role (Weick, 1995). Having opportunities to unpack dilemmas and challenges with a trusted mentor or coach will help the leader to develop confidence in their strategic thinking and will enable them to convey key issues and messages in a more assured way to their teams.

Often in new roles, new leaders feel that they cannot sound out their thinking as they are constantly being scrutinized by their teams. Having a safe, trusted space to explore creative ideas, and new ways of leading change and practice, helps them to develop ways forward in a more meaningful way.

Initial leadership conversations often centre on the leader's newly gained understanding of the context, work dynamics and team dynamics. This is often a period of sense making and working through the new issues that they are presented with. A helpful tool to use in these conversations is often to ask colleagues to outline a list of what they are noticing is a real strength in their team within the organisation, what is going well and what they are noticing in terms of what needs to be improved.

Table 9.1 A tool to help colleagues identify strengths and areas for improvement

Week (Reflect on what is your main learning.)	What is going well? (Review previous steps)	What needs to be refined?	What will be quick wins?	Who are the team members to involve?	How does the quick win align with the overall strategy?	What will be the potential impact?	What are the first steps to take?
1							
2							
3							
4							
5							

Through the learning conversations, the new leader can map their journey and reflect on their own new learning, what they feel is going well, what needs to be refined, what expertise they can tap into, who to involve and how to also think of quick wins, but they can also map out a longer-term approach over time by linking it to key strategies. The key with the above tool is to provide the new leader with a sense-making framework that celebrates success and identifies possible gaps, strategic ways forward and a way to carefully track their journey in line with a strategic vision and plan. This helps leaders to approach changes in a more reflective and reflexive way and enables them to be mindful of who they need to work with, and during learning conversations with mentors or coaches, they often also explore how to work with others more specifically. As the leader is growing in confidence, the mentor will need to recontract and start moving towards a coaching approach, to help facilitate the thinking for the coachee. It is a wonderful sign when this takes place, as the new leader will have a strong foundation to move forward in relation to their leadership journey and will have in place processes and practices that will help them to 'make sense' of their new context and to reflect on how to move forward with their teams on various issues they need to consider and explore.

Valuable Lessons and Experiences Shared by Experienced Mentors and Coaches

Krupa Patel shares her coaching journey as a BAMEed coach supporting women in education in the following case study:

> I have had the privilege to coach and mentor women and those from BAME backgrounds, in my school and as part of the BAMEed coaching community. I continue to be dubious about the term 'BAME'. As a British-born Indian and a headteacher, who, might I add, is a woman and a mother, I feel I have a multitude of layers I can offer. The power in offering myself in a relatable way has been the key in my coaching journey.
>
> I have been part of recruiting two women into my senior leadership team. Both have young children like me, and they are growing into women who believe that they can have it all!
>
> **Impact:**
> Mentoring and coaching these incredible women and modelling how to seek balance has been a real honour. We meet weekly. They are aware of the variety of coaching models and techniques we can use. Techniques include: the GROW model, BASIC model, visuals, mindful breathing and shadow work, such as that of the imposter. I am an avid user of Wilber's Integral AQAL model; this is a language which is now used to develop consciousness. The four areas include I, WE, IT and ITS. This model is now deeply embedded with the whole leadership team, and they use this within their departments.
>
> The impact so far has led to them wanting to share this level of mentoring and coaching transparently and equally, with positive challenges across all staff. As a result, with my school, we run coaching sessions in small groups every week. This has been a phenomenal shift as we are moving away from performance management to practitioner development. As we meet weekly,

> we are now entering our sessions deeply and very quickly. Therefore, each session is led by them, and their trust in not being judged has been pivotal in its success.
>
> Leading a team without ego (as much as I consciously can) as well as leading from behind has been the most humbling experience. I am not traditional in my leadership, and through coaching I encourage growing leaders to be who they want to be. The legacy is to enable all those that I meet on my journey to feel inspired to seek their purpose for their own pathways.
>
> I listen carefully and facilitate; they do the hard work and dig deep within themselves. If I am able to offer something that ignites growth and awareness of their true self and what they can achieve, that is plenty for me.
>
> I now aim to extend my love of coaching, be it as a coach or to consult on embedding a coaching culture in as many settings that allow me to.

Krupa's reflections in this case study demonstrate how powerful mentoring and coaching can be as a leadership strategy to enable others and to draw on lived experiences to make the journey more relatable. In the next section, explore the reflective task to consider how you can support others as a coach to unlock their potential.

> **Reflective Task**
>
> As a BAME coach or mentor, you will notice that this chapter aims to demonstrate how you can use existing frameworks and tools, such as a SWOT analysis, to help facilitate thinking for others. What other tools can you think of that you can draw on to help BAME mentees or coachees to shape their thinking, develop confidence and continue to make sense of their complex working environments? Some other examples are: reframing metaphors used, negative language used, journal reflections, three good things – practicing gratitude and positivity – and affirmations.
>
> Think of additional frameworks, strategies and techniques you can add to your coaching toolkit to facilitate the learning conversations you support in a variety of different ways.

Recommended Reading

Browne, A. (2020), *Lighting the Way: The Case for Ethical Leadership in Schools.* UK: Bloomsbury Education.

Shah, S. (2022), *Diversity, Inclusion and Belonging in Coaching: A Practical Guide*. UK: Kogan Page.

References

Bentley, R. (2020), 'Break-through conversations', Q595. Available at: https://q595-breakthrough-conversations.com/ (Accessed: 01. 09.2021).

Coalter, M. (2018), *Talent Architects: How to Make Your School a Great Place to Work*. Woodbridge: John Catt Publications.

Drake, D. B. (2017), *Narrative Coaching: The Definitive Guide to Bringing New Stories to Life*. UK: CNC Press.

Dweck, C. (2010), *Growth Mindset: Changing the Way You Think to Fulfil Your Potential*. USA: Robinson.

Elonga Mboyo, J. P. (2019), 'School leadership and Black and minority, ethnic career prospects in England: The choice between being a group prototype or deviant headteacher'. *Educational Management Administration and Leadership*, 1(47), pp. 110–28.

Francke, A. (2019), *Create A Gender-Balance Workplace*. UK: Penguin.

Garner, R. (2015), 'Headteachers urged to recruit more black and ethnic minority teachers', *The Independent*, 5th April.

Garvey, B. and Stokes, P. (2022), *Coaching and Mentoring: Theory and Practice*, 4th edn. UK: Sage Publishing.

Grant, V. (2014), *Staying A Head: The Stress Management Secrets of Successful School Leaders*. UK: Integrity Coaching.

Grenville-Cleave, B. (2016), *Positive Psychology: A Toolkit for Happiness, Purpose and Well-Being*. UK: Icon Books Ltd.

Kane, A., Lewis, R., and Yarker, J. (2021), 'The development of the Embodied, Dynamic and Inclusive (EDI) model of self-confidence; a conceptual model for use in executive coaching'. *International Coaching Psychology Review*. Spring2021, Vol. 16 Issue 1, pp. 6–21. 16p., Database: Psychology and Behavioral Sciences Collection.

Kostic, A. and Chadee, D. (2015), *The Social Psychology of Nonverbal Communication*. UK: Palgrave.

Oberholzer, L. (2019), *Developing Future Black Minority, Ethnic (BME) Leader's Self-Efficacy through Mentoring and Coaching*. UK: CollectiveEd. Available at: https://www.bameednetwork.com/wp-content/uploads/2019/11/CollectivED-Working-Papers.pdf (Accessed: 01. 09.2021).

Oberholzer, L. (2021), *Is There a Glass Ceiling in Higher Education?* UK: Sage. Available at: https://perspectivesblog.sagepub.com/blog/books/is-there-a-glass-ceiling-in-higher-education (Accessed: 01.09.2021).

Porritt, V. (2021), Issues of gender and diversity: deliberate disruption, Presentation delivered at the IPDA Conference, November 2021, Marginalised voices in contemporary times: Addressing inequities through professional learning and education.

Porritt, V. and Featherstone, K. (2019), *10% Braver: Inspiring Women to Lead Education*. UK: Sage Publishing.

Seligman, M. (2011), PERMA—A Well-Being Theory by Martin Seligman. *Free Press*. Available at: https://www.habitsforwellbeing.com/perma-a-well-being-theory-by-martin-seligman (Accessed: 01.09.2021).

Small, I. (2019), *The Unexpected Leader: Exploring the Real Nature of Values, Authenticity and Moral Purpose in Education*. UK: Independent Thinking Press.

Weick, K. (1995), *Sensemaking in Organisations*. London: Sage.

Conclusion

Lizana Oberholzer and Derek Boyle

As authors we set out to provide guidance on how you can support colleagues on their initial career journey, leadership journeys and different learning trajectories as teachers. We were very fortunate to also have the expertise from a wide range of school leaders and experts in the sector to draw on to enable us to reflect on what guidance and support are needed to ensure that we fully equip mentors and coaches in their role to support others in becoming the best they can be for the learners we support in our schools and education contexts.

It is fair to say that coaching and mentoring, as an evolving field in education, will continue to develop, and the guidance provided in this book is not an exclusive outline of what can be done or achieved. Instead, we are hoping that the book will become part of the discourse, advocating the important role of mentoring and coaching in teacher development and professional learning throughout a teaching career. It is our hope that mentoring and coaching would not be utilized as performative tools but, instead, that it is used as a force for good to encourage learning conversations and collaborative professional dialogues with others. Coaching and mentoring can make a profound difference to the learning journey of a teacher, and excellent support can ensure that we retain those wonderful educators and teacher learners needed on a daily basis in the classroom. Kindness, support and understanding go a long way. It is vital to ensure that teachers are looked after; as Campbell (2021) pointed out, a negative work environment for teachers becomes a negative and toxic environment for learners. It is therefore imperative that we continue to strive to focus on developing others, making use of supportive practices to enable them to unlock their potential and flourish.

At the time of writing this book, coaching and mentoring started to play a more prominent role in continuing to support early careers teachers, and support is also provided in a similar way on the national professional qualifications. We felt it was timely to share these ideas and practices with others to extend our learning beyond our own practice.

Teaching is one of the most rewarding careers one can have, and being part of developing teachers and future leaders is an even greater privilege. Coaching and mentoring approaches and practices also develop effective leadership skills which leaders can draw on in future as they develop skills in active listening, empathy and body language, as well as help leaders to develop greater emotional intelligence and self-awareness. In communities where collaborative professional conversations take place, learning is valued and the voices of all are heard and appreciated, and in turn, these new cultures of learning contribute to creating more effective and supportive learning cultures for our young people and children.

Coaching and mentoring advocate that we listen to the needs of the individual we support; if we do that well, we provide an opportunity to help someone to flourish and to enjoy teaching and leadership in education as fulfilling careers. In turn, we also ensure that future learners have leaders who are empathetic, kind and supportive and who always strive to meet the needs of every learner.

Index

action learning sets (RQT) 66–8
AD HOC programme 95
adult learners 14, 24–5, 45
affective processes 107
Association or School and College Leader (ASCL), Ethical framework 122

BAMEed 157, 159–62, 166
Barnett, K. 105–6
BASIC coaching method 15, 160
Beauchamp, G. 108
Beck, D. E. 133
Bentley, R. 141, 143–4, 157
Berry, J. 132–3
Bibi, Y. 141
Bird, J. 125
Black, Asian and minority ethnic (BAME) colleagues 155
  to apply for leadership roles 161–2
  case study 166–7
  challenges often face 158
  coaching and mentoring 157–8
  from diverse backgrounds 156–7
  to drive goals 160–1
  embrace new role with confidence 163–4
  female representation 156
  moving forward with career goals/focus 158–60
  to prepare for interview process 162–3
  reflective task 167
  tool to identify strengths/areas for improvement 165
Blanchard, K. 62, 81, 85, 102, 108
Bleach, K. 45, 47, 51
British Minority Ethnic (BME) female representation 138

Bromley Schools' Collegiate School Centred Initial Teacher Training (SCITT) course 38
Browne, A. 68, 104
Bruner, J. S. 36, 38
Buck, A. 15, 18, 64, 88, 143
  BASIC coaching method 15, 160
  mentoring continuum 64
  trusting learning relationship 16

Caffarella, R. S. 25
Cambers, N. 139
Cameron, E. 163
Campbell, J. 169
career progression 74, 161
Carter Review 2, 12, 45
Chadee, D. 163
Chartered College of Teaching 53, 70
Chartered Institute of Personnel and Development (CIPD) 138
client 5
Clutterbuck, D. 6, 10, 15, 28, 30, 49, 65, 82, 103, 144
coachee 5, 7, 10, 12, 15, 18, 82, 103, 108, 113, 124, 134, 141, 144, 150, 160–1
  BAMEed 157, 161, 167
  needs 2, 16–17, 140–3, 157–9, 162
coaching 1–2, 5–8, 15, 47, 55–7, 62–3, 65, 80–1, 84–5, 91, 101–3, 116, 124, 138, 140, 143, 149, 155, 157–8, 164, 169–70
Coalter, M. 62, 155
cognitive leadership approaches 80, 138
cognitive processes 106
cognitive skills 163
The CollectivED Advanced Mentoring programme 8–9
CollectiveEd Dilemma Based Model 110

Index

Connor, M. 6, 10, 103, 140
considerations (mentoring/coaching) 10–16, 82, 97
   mentor relationship's phases 10, 11
   standards 13
contextual coaching 142
continuum (mentoring/coaching) 18, 28, 61, 63–4, 68, 74, 80, 82, 84, 102–3, 144–5, 149, 157, 162
coordination processes 108
Covey, M. R. 25
Cowan, C. W. 133
Cowley, S. 139
Crawford, M. 88
critically reflective practice, model 36–7, 68, 112–13
cultural norms 83
Curee's National Framework for Mentoring and Coaching 7

data analysis 14, 147
Davis, M. 40
decision-making process 88, 125, 131
Department for Education (DfE) 1, 25, 44
   Governance Handbook and Competency Framework 112
   lack of BAME leaders 156
developing agency in teachers 65
dilemma based coaching model 110
directing-coaching-supporting-delegating pathway 81
directive approach 7–8, 11, 18, 103
diversity 16, 116, 155–6
Door, V. 12, 14, 25, 45, 51
Drake, D. B. 142–4, 157–9
Dreyfus model 11, 16, 27, 52, 62–3, 80, 82, 104, 163
   of adult skill acquisition 81
Dreyfus, S. 11, 102
Durrant, J. 65

Early Careers Framework (ECF) 1, 13, 44–5, 47
Early Careers Teachers (ECTs) 1, 9–10, 43–5, 61, 63
   behaviour management 53
   case study 56–7

   coaching strategies to support mentees 55
   development challenges for NQTs 52–3
   expectations 49–50
   facilitating thinking (feedback) 54
   learning framework 47
   limbic system 54
   mentoring and coaching 46–7, 55
   mentor meetings 50–2
   observation and feedback 53
   reflections 55–7
   and School Educational Leadership development 1
   standardized agenda 56
   targets and goals 54–5
Early Professional Development (EPD), Training Schools 44
educational change 9
Education Endowment Foundation 70
Education White Paper 24
effective mentoring 2, 9–10, 23, 41, 56
effective teaching and learning 69–70
empathy 28, 143, 170
enquiry-based learning 36
European Mentoring and Coaching Council (EMCC) 5, 141, 159

Featherstone, K. 138–9
Francke, A. 155
French, M. 117
Furlong, J. 14, 52
future career development 1

Garner, R. 156
Garvey, B. 155
Gornall, S. 125
Graves, C. W. 133
Green, M. 163
Grenville-Cleave, B. 160
GROW (goal, reality, options, will) model 16, 36, 160
The Guardian 145
guidance 5–6, 8, 11, 14–15, 25, 28, 44, 47, 50, 68, 74, 143, 150, 157, 169

Hagger, H. 51
headship 132, 147–9

Index

headteachers 121, 137, 166
    career development plans 130
    case for change 122–3
    case studies 132–4
    with challenging issues 129
    with challenging outcomes and Ofsted 129
    coaching research 9
    communicating vision 123–5
    on curriculum provided 128
    facilitate thinking 130
    with human resource issues 129
    to lead change 125–7
    managing stakeholders 127–8
    well-being and workload 131
    on working effectively with school budgets 129
Headteacher's Standards 122
Heidi and Howard effect 139, 146
Hersey, P. 108
Hewitt, R. 138
Higher Education Statistics Agency (HESA) 138
higher education workforce 138
Hollweck, T. 142
Hughes, M. 6

Ibarra, H. 25
inclusion 9, 156
Initial Teacher Education (ITE) 2, 9–10, 15
Initial Teacher Training/Trainees (ITT) 1, 6, 12, 15, 24, 39, 45–8, 53, 69, 147–8, 150–1
    Coordinator 16, 24, 56
    Core Framework 1, 13–14, 44, 48
International Coaching Federation (ICF) 141
International Professional Development Association (IPDA) 156

Kahn, P. 36
Keyes, C. L. M. 98
Kline, N. 1, 143
Knapper, C. K. 56
Knight, J. 1, 18
    trusting learning relationship 16
Kostic, A. 163

Lane, G. 6, 10, 15, 28, 30, 49, 65, 82, 103, 144
leadership 1, 8–10, 12, 14, 16, 26, 32, 46–7, 66, 96, 102, 107, 114, 116, 125, 170. *See also* middle leaders/leadership (ML); senior leadership/Senior Leadership Team (SLT)
    BAME colleagues 158–62
    incubators 65, 67
    strategic 88
    time 130
    women in (*see* women in leadership)
leadership roles (RQT) 61, 71
    contributing to team meetings 71–2
    needs of team, understanding 72
    shadowing line management meetings 72
listening 15, 28, 39, 55, 89, 122, 143, 150, 170
Lofthouse, R. M. 1–2, 8, 142

Market Review 25
Maslow, A. 28
Maynard, T. 52
McCormick, J. 105–6
McIntyre, D. 51
meeting (mentor/coaching) 30–1, 50–2, 83, 104, 112
mentee 5–7, 9–10, 15, 28, 37, 40–1, 47, 49, 54, 56, 65, 73, 82, 108, 121–2, 124, 140, 142, 157, 160, 162–3
    anxiety and imposter syndrome 104–5
    to become confident in classroom 68–9
    career development of 114–15
    consideration 30
    development phases of 52
    and mentor relationship 7, 10–12, 15, 45, 50
    needs 2, 10, 13–17, 25–6, 55, 148, 157–9
    recognizing scope 104
    trusting learning relationship 18, 157
mentoring 1–2, 5–10, 13–15, 23–4, 40, 44–5, 55, 62–3, 76, 80–1, 84–5, 89, 91, 101–2, 105, 108, 122, 125, 138, 140, 147–51, 155, 157–8, 161–3, 166, 169–70
    guidance and advice 6
    levels of 51–2
mentor relationship 6, 10, 25, 52, 65, 75, 122
    Dreyfus model 11, 16

mentee and 7, 10–12, 15, 45, 50
    prompt questions 75–6
Merrill, R. R. 25
Mezirow, J. 56
middle leaders/leadership (ML) 62, 74, 79–80, 103, 116
    active listening 89
    to address difficult situations 87–8
    case study 95–6
    on developing career plan 92–3
    expectations 83
    facilitating thinking 95
    to lead change 85–6
    to lead on appraisals 91
    to lead strategically 88–90
    line management of 80
    mentoring and coaching 84–5
    novice phase 81
    reflective task 82, 84
    self-awareness of negative bias 88
    on senior leadership roles 93–4
    SMART data to shape planning 90–1
    to support teams 86–7
    Type A 80, 83
    Type B 80, 83–4
    Type C 81, 83–4
    Type D 81, 83, 85
    well-being 96
modelling, teacher 25
models of coaching 7–8, 14–15, 82, 101, 103, 110, 142–4, 159–60, 166
models of mentoring 14, 16, 65, 82
Moor, H. 43
motivation 47, 65, 107
motivational processes 107
Mullin, S. 115
Multi-Academy Trust (MAT) 102, 113, 121–2
Myatt, M. 95

narrative coaching model 141–4, 146, 158–9
National College of School Leadership (NCLT), The Role and Purpose of middle leaders in Schools 90
National Mentor Standards 25

National Professional Qualification (NPQ) 44, 61
    for School Leaders 8
National Professional Qualification in Middle Leadership (NPQML) 74
national standards (ITT) 12, 24
nature 5
newly qualified teachers (NQTs) 36, 43–4, 47, 56–7, 73–4, 141, 151
    development challenges 52–3
Nolan Principles of public life 102, 122
non-directive coaching approach 6–8, 15, 18

Oberholzer, L. 147, 156, 158–9
Ofsted 2, 10, 45, 129
O'Rourke, K. 36
Osho, S. 138, 156

Pain, M. 122
paraphrasing 55, 89, 143, 162
Passmore, J. 141
Patel, K. 166–7
Peacock, A. 139
peer-mentoring 107
PERMA model 34–5, 160
Pierce, K. 9
Pokora, J. 6, 10, 103, 140
Porritt, V. 138–9, 145, 147–8, 156
Porter, S. 73
positive psychology 34–5
practical guidance 15
The Princes' Teaching Institute, *Find Your Voice!* 117
principal teacher 122
professional learners 1–2, 16–18, 44, 46, 48, 55, 68, 103
professional learning 8–9, 24, 35, 46, 156, 169
professional mentor 56
Professional Tutor 16
psychological well-being (middle leader) 97–8

Ratcliff-Daffron, S. 25
recently qualified teacher (RQT) 61
    action learning sets 66–8
    case study 73–4
    coaching/mentoring 63–4

on developing career pathways 71
development goals, supporting with 64–6
effective teaching and learning 69–70
expectations 63
facilitating thinking time 73
leadership roles 71–3
mentee, helping 68–9
well-being, workload and retention 75–6
reflective practitioner 31–2
reflexive mentor 75, 105
reflexive practices 25
re-image 8, 117
Roberts, A. 6
Ryff, C. D. 97

safe space 1, 10, 103, 141–2, 149–50, 157, 161, 163–4
Sandberg, J. 138–9, 141, 145–7
School Workforce Census 137
self-awareness 88, 108, 159, 170
self-efficacy 156, 158, 162
self-reflection 24, 29, 31, 33, 82, 113, 130
Seligman, M. 34, 160. *See also* PERMA model
senior leadership/Senior Leadership Team (SLT) 16, 26, 32, 53, 56, 62, 68, 79–80, 85, 91, 101, 130, 141, 145, 166
    to address difficult situations 109–11
    career development of mentee 114–15
    case study 115–18
    developing learning relationships 103
    expectations 102
    facilitating thinking 112–13
    to lead change 105–8
    mentee anxiety and imposter syndrome 104–5
    mentee role, scope 104
    mentoring and coaching 102–4
    middle leaders on 94
    reflective task 106
    well-being 113–14
    to work effectively with school governors/trustees 111–12
    to work well with parents and stakeholders 111
    to work with teams 108–9

senior lead for staff development (SLSD) 16
Senior Mentor 16
Silver, M. 133
Sinek, S. 124
situational leadership model 81, 108
skills 6–7, 9, 12, 14, 16, 64, 108, 116, 155, 161–3, 170
    acquisition 6, 11, 47, 52, 63
    cognitive leadership 138, 163
    development 16, 46
    impact 117
    inspiration 117
    legacy 117–18
Small, I. 158, 161
SMART target 29
social well-being (middle leader) 98
Special Education Needs and Disabilities (SEND) 43, 133–4
speed coaching 140
sponsor 5, 7, 17
staff development (schools) 8–10, 16, 118
stakeholders 88, 91, 124, 126, 133
    under primary grouping 127
    under secondary grouping 128
    senior leaders to work well with parents and 111
Starr, J. 6
Steare, R., ethicability 110, 149–50
Stokes, P. 155
strategic leadership 88–90
summary 50, 53, 55, 89, 143, 150
support 1–2, 5–9, 13–16, 30, 35, 43–5, 47, 52, 61, 64, 70, 74, 80, 150, 169
    BAME colleagues 155, 157, 160, 163
    coaching strategies to mentees 55
    future women into leadership 140–1, 147
    headteacher 130
    middle leader 81, 85–8, 95
    RQT's needs 62
    RQT with development goals 64–6
    senior leaders 103, 106, 115
SWOT (strengths, weaknesses, opportunities and threats) analysis 62, 159–60, 167

talent management 62, 67, 115
Teacher Development Agency (TDA) 44

teachers and educators 1–2, 8–10, 12, 16, 25, 43–4, 46–7, 62–3, 65, 68, 86, 111, 137, 150–1, 169–70. *See also* trainee teachers
teacher-student relationship 35
Teacher Wellbeing Index 43
'Teacher Well-Being: Its Effects on Teaching Practice and Student Learning' 35
teaching 46, 48, 69–70, 151, 170
Teaching Assistant (TA) 151
Teaching/Teachers' Standards 2, 32, 38, 44–6, 48
Thomson, B. 6–7, 64, 124, 143, 157
Tice, J. 31
trainee teachers 23–4, 46
   case study 40–1
   from dependence to independence 35–6
   empathy 28
   expectations 24–5
   facilitating their thinking 36–8
   internal challenges 27
   mentor/coaching meeting 30–1
   needs of mentee 25–6
   observations and feedback 32–3
   positive mindset, developing 33–4
   positive psychology 34–5
   professional growth and development phases 52
   reflective practitioner 31–2
   targets and goals 28–30
   well-being 38–9
Tsoukas, H. 141

UK Aid 139
universities, Coaching and Mentoring Programmes 10

Vare, P. 8

Wathen, N. 9
well-being and work-life balance 9, 28
   headteachers 131
   middle leaders 85, 96–8
   RQT 75–6
   senior leadership 113–14
Westerhof, G. J. 98
Whitmore, J. 36, 143
Wigston, I., 'The Magic in the Space Between' 133
Wilber, K., Integral AQAL model 166
Williams, A. 52
WomenEd 137, 141, 145, 147, 150, 156
women in leadership 137–9, 158, 166
   case study 150–1
   challenges women often face 145
   coaching and mentoring 144–5
   during Covid-19 138
   from cradle to headship 147–9
   to drive goals 147
   embrace new role with confidence 149–50
   forward with career goals and focus 146
   learning conversations 140–1
   and management workforce 138
   narrative coaching 141–4
   sharing stories 141–2

Yamina (professional mentor) 56–7
Yusuf, B. 141